A Nay for Effort

Lessons from the School of Life

Dan Bain

This book is dedicated to the teachers of the world, especially those saints who had me in their classes.

I still have nightmares where I forgot to show up all year; do you still have nightmares where I remembered?

Class Schedule

Acknowledgments

Mom and Dad, this journey wouldn't have been possible without your support. I think it started in 1973, when you gave me my first library card – and paid my first overdue fine a month later. You've since paid for my education, a word processor and plenty of mistakes. Thanks for all of it. Sorry I still haven't learned to return my books on time.

Dan and Gina, each of you took a chance in giving a column to an unknown like me. Dan, I can only hope that's not why you took the buy-out. Gina, you continue to give me more credit than I deserve, but far be it from me to dispel your notions. Thank you both for the opportunities.

Unca Don! You and the Taffies have provided unlimited moral support and set innumerable positive examples. Plus, you're just a whole lot of fun. Thanks for sharing your wisdom, your friendship and your laughter. (And thanks to Loco Lu for sharing your space.)

Walter, you might not know it, but you were the first one to motivate me. It started with your email replies that said, "Put this one in a book!" So I did. I thank you and the other Walters through the years who have encouraged me from afar.

Lastly, to Sweetie, Doodlebug and Sugarbear – I don't know where to start or how to describe everything I need to thank you for. You've been unwilling participants in all of this; while I crave an audience, you shun it. This has led to countless sacrifices on your part, not the least of which have been your privacy and dignity. Thank you for tolerating that in support of my dream; I hope I can support your dreams as a result. Please know that I've never written about you to belittle you; it's always been my intent that I should be the only one who comes off looking like an idiot. I hope I've succeeded. I write about you in adoration, not mockery. Thank you for being my inspiration, my supporters and my life. I love you guys.

Foreword

When humor goes, there goes civilization.
- Erma Bombeck

I believe there are no accidental meetings, and that was the case when I met Dan Bain. Both parents of children in first grade and volunteering to help with a school event; Dan offering to write an article and I offering to publish it... the rest is history.

I quickly learned Dan is a phenomenal writer, but more importantly, he's funny. His talent for sharing life experiences as a husband, father and son, I compare to columnist and author Erma Bombeck. Dan, like Bombeck, chronicles ordinary life with eloquence and humor. He exposes his missteps with others and his own shortcomings in a way that we can all relate to and laugh.

You should write big stuff for a national audience – perhaps a book. Congratulations on your award. You deserve recognition. Make us all laugh – we need to laugh.
- Don, a reader from San Diego

Dan's only shortcoming as a writer is his modesty; it took lots of prodding by me and others to convince him to compile his award-winning columns into this book. I know the addition of Dan's column "Bain's Beat" to *Midtown Magazine* is one of the wisest decisions I've made as a publisher.

I hope as you read this book, you will be inspired to laugh at yourself and others more freely. As Erma said, "If you can't make it better, laugh at it."

Gina Pearce Stephens,
Publisher

Introduction

This book actually has nothing to do with education – at least not in any traditional sense of the word. I apologize if you purchased it expecting funny stories about school, as you may be disappointed on both counts.

Education was more of a theme for this book than a topic. Chances are, it will never be a topic for me. I'll never write about my K-12 days, at least, as most of those memories tend toward the unpleasant side. I made lifelong friends there whom I still enjoy seeing on Facebook, but beyond that I can't say I enjoyed school.

Especially gym. I hated gym.

For 13 years, school amounted to a daily dose of humiliation – the unpleasant nicknames, the struggle with hormones, the threat of bullies, the sense of not belonging, the constant mistakes I made to the great delight of those who witnessed my stupidity.

I adapted by developing the only defense available to me – a sense of humor. It helped me make friends, albeit not with any of my teachers. I'm afraid school was probably no more pleasant for them than it was for me. I wasn't a bad student, I was just a bad...*participant*, let's say.

My teachers never understood that my behavior was nothing personal. It was never meant as a barrier against them specifically; rather, it was a barrier against *everything*.

It took me a long time to realize humor needn't be a barrier at all. Today I use it more like a filter – something that won't block the humiliation, but can certainly change my perception of it. I had to leave school and grow up a little (debatably) before I understood this.

And I realized something else about those days – I'm not as far-removed from them as I thought. I'm still learning, still questioning my grades and still annoying the people in charge, who still wish I would sit down, shut up and for God's sake, let them teach me a thing or two.

I still struggle with the rest of it, too – the unpleasant nicknames, the struggle with hormones, the threat of bullies, the sense of not belonging, the constant mistakes I make to the great delight of those who witness my stupidity.

Only now, I filter every bit of it. That way, the lessons don't hurt nearly as much. In fact, they're sort of fun. I've captured some of them on the following pages. Think of it as my continuing education – these stories represent lessons I learned long after leaving school, but I'm amazed to look back and recognize the patterns from those days that still repeat today. All of the old subjects are here.

Except gym. I hated gym.

Thanks,
Dan

A Nay for Effort

Period 1:
Language Arts

Man developed language to satisfy
his deep need to complain.

– Lily Tomlin

Doodlebug Drops the F-Bomb

Teach your child to hold his tongue;
he'll learn fast enough to speak.

– Benjamin Franklin

O ur six-year-old loves words. He practically covets them, keeping my old Collegiate Dictionary in his room just in case the urge strikes to learn more. There are times, though, when he prefers to simply *play* with his words.

This is usually harmless fun, but once in a while becomes a dangerous game – usually when we're irrevocably in public. Such was the case last Sunday night at Bojangles'....

Like most six-year-olds, he enjoys being silly. He's not so proud of being intelligent that he won't take time to act otherwise. On the night in question, he was intentionally mispronouncing words – something he enjoys doing from time to time. He'll just decide out of the blue to pronounce most of his words with the same incorrect beginning letter.

On this particular night, the letter "F" held the position of honor. I should have known this would lead to trouble; I'd received a big clue several nights before, when he was effing up his words in a mock interview he'd asked me to host.

"What's your name?"

"Foodlebug!"

"Okay, Doodlebug, what's your favorite thing to eat for dinner?"

"Facaroni and Feese!"

"How about for dessert?"

"Feminems!"

"Do you like school?"

"Fes!"

"Who's your favorite person there?"

"My feacher!"

"What's your favorite class?"

"Fart!"

We broke into giggles over that one, and the interview was over. So, I thought, was the game – until I told him I needed to go outside and work in the yard.

"Daddy? Can I come out with you, to falk around?"

I stopped in my tracks; he had me at "falk."

"Do what??"

"I said I want to falk around for a while."

"Umm...."

"I won't go far; I'll just falk around the yard while you're working."

"Oh! You want to *walk* around! S-sure you can, but do me a favor, and let's not repeat that to any neighbors you happen to see."

"Fokay!"

I falked out the door, glad to know I had fisunderstood what he meant – and finking the issue was dead. Until Funday night at Fojangles'.

We were just digging into our FoBerry Fiscuit when it began – he and his little brother were looking out the window at New Bern Avenue, watching the vehicles speed past. As they did so, Doodlebug narrated to any diners who could hear him – of which there were, unfortunately, many.

A car drove by. "Hey, look! A far!"

Next came a bus. "Fuss! It's a big fuss!"

Then a tractor trailer rumbled by. "Factor failer, everybody! Some people call it a fig rig. It has 18 fires, you know."

I smiled at him, paying no mind to the traffic. If I had, I might have noticed the next vehicle – a Ford F-150. Which would have been fine, had that been the name by which Doodlebug knows that particular vehicle. One can replace the first sound in "Ford" with an "F" and have little or no effect. (Also, little or no embarrassment to one's parents.) Not so when one knows that vehicle simply as "truck."

But none of this occurred to me as I gave myself over to the euphoric rush of my sweet tea. My mind was clouded to the fact that he was replacing not just single letters, but also consonant blends such as the "tr" in "trailer" – coincidentally, the same consonant blend in "truck" – with the single "f" sound. Yep, he was about to go fricative on me....

I think you know what came out of his mouth next. Propriety and spam filters prevent me from using the specific word, but we all know it. Everyone at Bojangles' knew it, too.

That was evident by the multiple shocked reactions when he shouted the word with great enthusiasm – and volume to match – as the truck raced by. I shot sweet tea through my nose and watched my wife give herself whiplash as she dropped her biscuit and spun her head to look at him.

"What did you say?!?"

He knew by the tone of her voice that there was no acceptable answer to that question. I could tell from the look in his eyes – he knew he'd done something off the scale of the bad-meter, but he had no idea what it was. So I have to give him points for trying to answer her – that was the only thing he knew to do at that point, and the poor kid had no idea that it could only get him in more trouble.

"I said 'fu-'"

"DON'T! SAY IT! AGAIN!!!"

"Why? What's wrong, Mommy?"

I stepped in at this point, fully accustomed to our tag-team routine of answering for one another.

"Doodlebug, you probably didn't know this, but that word you said? It's a bad word. In fact, it's not just any bad word, it's the *mother* of all bad words – probably the worst word on the list of bad words, possibly the worst word in the history of words."

"Why? What does it mean, Daddy?"

"Er..." I stopped to sip more tea as my wife tagged me out.

"Never mind what it means," she said. "That's how bad it is, we can't even say what it means."

"Well, if you don't know what it means, that's okay; it's probably in my dictionary. I'll look it up when we get home."

"No, you don't need to look it up."

"Is it a noun or a verb?"

"Yes," I answered, "and sometimes, a gerund!"

"DAN!"

"Listen, Doodlebug," I said, working hard to get us both out of trouble now. "We know you've probably never heard that word before, and that's a good thing. You didn't know you

4

were saying a bad word, so you're not in trouble. But if you want to stay out of trouble, you'll forget that word even exists. Don't look it up, don't ask about it, don't say it any more. Fokay?"

"Fokay, Faddy."

"Fattaboy."

We collected our things and left, under the glaring watch of a group of octogenarian Southern Baptist women who'd come in for their post-service repast, and had been trying to say a group blessing when Doodlebug had announced the truck's untimely arrival. I was tempted to stop and say, "You ought to hear him when he's really mad" but I figured I was in enough trouble already.

The rest of the night passed without incident. We drove to our fome, were greeted by our fat, and put the boys to fed. There was, however, one last bit of funfinished business.

Once he was asleep, I snuck into Doodlebug's room with a flashlight, searching for the fook in question. I was carrying a fair of fissors.

I'll never own up to what I did, but suffice it to say – if he ever needs to look up a word that falls between "frontal bone" and "fugitive," he's out of, umm, *luck*....

- March 2008

5

Putting the Cart Before the Truth

*The minute you read something you can't understand,
you can almost be sure it was drawn up by a lawyer.*

— Will Rogers

T he truth hurts. But not as much as a rogue Lego on the bathroom floor at 3am. That's a double pain – the initial jolt to the sole, followed by a one-footed hop and probable stumble into something else painful, like a sharp countertop or pointy towel rack.

Sometimes the truth hurts so much, people feel they have to soften it with euphemisms. I recently contemplated this while wandering the aisles of a store, shopping for a new pointy towel rack.

For legal reasons, I shouldn't name the store I'm targeting. Suffice it to say, it was one of those huge, discount stores that have become so prevalent – you can hardly throw your wallet without hitting one nowadays.

I started my contemplations to pass the time during the first 30 minutes of my shopping expedition, also known as searching for a parking spot. After I found one, I thumbed a ride to the store's main entrance, bought a vat of popcorn and began my tour of duty. An hour later, I'd searched half the store when I felt nature's call. Fortunately I'd left a trail of kernels and was able to find my way back to Customer Service, aka the food court and restrooms.

I was just about to walk into the men's room when I spotted a perfect example of the euphemisms I'd been contemplating – there, among the other 57 protective disclaimers nailed to the door, was this inexplicable proclamation: "Carts prohibited in restroom, for your safety."

That's nothing but an out-and-out lie. Shopping carts in bathrooms are generally not a safety issue, unless the floors are electrified or there's a man-eating troll, who hates squeaky wheels, sleeping in one of the stalls.

No, there's some greater truth at play there.

I'm fully qualified to discuss how words can be used to hide the truth, having worked in PR. The sign is an obvious euphemism, an attempt to hide the truth from its natural predators – lawyers.

The word "euphemism" is based on an ancient Greek phrase meaning "lawyer repellent." This technique should be used only when the truth is in mortal danger. That's where PR comes in; their job is to camouflage the truth in order to keep it safe. Ironically, they rely on a method that's also used by lawyers – it has four letters, and begins with "s."

That's right, it's "spin." What word were you thinking?

Anyway, the predatory nature of lawyers forces the rest of us to put such a spin on words that we essentially knock the truth out of them. That, or hide it behind a jumbled morass of words so confusing as to throw the lawyers off its scent, but that usually happens in boardrooms rather than restrooms.

The sign on the restroom door is simply spin, and I've used my counter-rotation technique to narrow its true meaning down to three possibilities:

1. "Carts prohibited in restroom, for health reasons. Sure, we have a schedule on the wall claiming that we check it every 15 minutes and clean it every hour, but do you know who does that? It's Randy, the waste of air who took a summer job here in lieu of community service. You might have seen him out front, t-boning minivans with the cart train or eating grapes in our produce section. Doesn't instill much confidence in our sanitary conditions, does he? You know what's in that white spray bottle he uses to 'clean' this place? We're almost sure it's bong water. Yep, this restroom is pretty much a petri dish. We don't want our carts spreading e-coli, foot-in-mouth, mad cow, swine flu, avian flu, Asian flu, the flu, bi-polar disorder, radiation sickness, scabies, rabies, babies or anything else one might get from contact with the unclean surfaces in this room. If that happens, someone might become ill after having placed their processed frozen stuff resembling food into a tainted cart; they could sue us for upwards of five

gazillion dollars, forcing our CEO to give up half of this year's bonus."

2. "Carts prohibited in restroom, as a theft-deterrent. Many of our shoppers are hardened criminals and we can't afford to give you the benefit of the doubt. We caught a guy in here the other day, trying to ram his cart through the wall to the parking lot. By the time our security teen caught him, the cart had accordioned up on itself and on the guy's fingers, effectively maiming him for life. All for a Clay Aiken CD and a pack of Bubblicious. He could have just stuck those in his pocket and walked around the security sensors, like Randy does every night. But we can't accuse you, or you'll sue. Last year, we caught a lady carrying a set of golf clubs out of here in her purse. When we confronted her, she claimed they were hers and that they'd been in her purse – price tags and all – when she came into the store. She sued us for character defamation and won ten quadrillion dollars. Our CEO had to sell his private jet on eBay. That's almost worse than when some guy sued us because he was offended by the 'XXL' tag on the muumuu he bought from us. We had to change all of the tags to say, 'Big-boned, but with a nice personality.' It took Randy months with a Sharpie to accomplish that, but at least he discovered that one of the muumuus was torn, and now has some rags to use when he cleans the restroom."

3. "Carts prohibited in restroom, as they will probably block access. Unless you angle that behemoth just right, it will stick in the doorway like a cork. Chances are, there's a kid behind you doing the Dr. Pepper dance from the 20-ouncer he stole from our cooler earlier. If you block his way, he might have an accident right in front of aisle 83, the one with the pretty cashier who's also his babysitter and the older sister of his best friend. The kid will undoubtedly be traumatized by the humiliation and his parents will sue us for 25 susquitillion dollars, causing our CEO's head to implode. Plus, Randy will have to end his smoking break prematurely in order to clean up the mess, which will

make him angry. You know the car vandalism in the parking lot? That's what Randy does when he's happy. You don't want to make Randy angry. We think he's still carrying the stun gun he lifted from our 'Seasonal Recreation' display."

Hmm. In light of that threat, maybe the carts really *are* banned for your safety. Guess I was wrong.

Sorry to have wasted your time; if you feel recompense is due, just have your liars contact my liars.

- June 2007

English Major Will Work for Pie

To get maximum attention, it's hard to beat a good, big mistake.
- Joseph R. Alsop, Jr.

I remember that summer night after my Freshman year when I told my parents I was changing majors from Computer Science to English. After they came to, they expressed their concerns – they were worried I'd never find employment. But I've disproved them by now, having been through countless jobs over the years.

There are plenty of jobs out there for other English majors, too, since no one else can or will do them. Ironically, my previous Computer Science classmates are back in the market, having had their jobs outsourced. And because they've never learned to communicate with anything human, they create ridiculous grammatical errors all over the place.

Don't believe me? Look around. It's as if we've become a world without a proofreader. Most of the errors are found in signs at businesses; their owners should hire English majors to review everything they intend to hang on their walls. For example, a friend of mine recently saw this sign at a store: *Dog's Welcome.*

If they meant to imply that all dogs are welcome, they need to erase the apostrophe, which is used for possessives and contractions rather than plurals. Leaving it in creates numerous other interpretations....

Could be a true possessive and they're warning us that a "Dog's Welcome" is what we will receive if we go into that store. (In which case I'd pass, not wanting a salesclerk to wag his tail, drool on me and sniff me in inappropriate places.)

Or maybe it's a true contraction and they meant to say, "Dog is welcome." (Only one, though.) Sounds rather Slavic, da? "Dog is welcome, but Moose and Squirrel must die, Boris." That, or they're big Duane Chapman fans.

Lastly, it could mean that a dyslexic was preparing for the Second Coming.

Another friend shared this beauty, which he saw at a Chick-fil-A: *It's "our pleasure" to refill your drink.*

Quotation marks are meant to enclose either direct quotes or figurative language. Since there was no source cited for the insightful quote of "our pleasure," one can assume the phrase is figurative. (In which case I'd be pretty skeptical of their intentions and probably eschew the refill.)

But what else can we expect, grammatically, from the franchise that purports a single letter "A" makes the long "ey" sound? Sorry, but that letter as a syllable would be nothing more than a schwa, meaning the franchise should really be pronounced, "Chick-fil-uh."

I'm not even going to talk about the people who misuse the ellipse...on...their...signs. When I see them, I have to wonder if William Shatner dictated the words.

Last fall, my favorite McDonald's posted its employment needs and seasonal menu offerings on the same sign without any punctuation, resulting in this gem: *NOW HIRING MAN-AGERS & CREW PUMPKIN PIE.*

Can you imagine how the job interview for a pumpkin pie might go? "Well, we need someone with a crusty personality, but who's not afraid to be sweet inside. Your role will fit within a typical box."

A sign over a local buffet informed me that "Food must be cook before eating." Either they're cannibals or they don't know the past participle. Plus, it's just insulting – do they think their customers are stupid enough to eat anything that hasn't been cooked? (Other than sushi.)

I recently found the word "Broke" taped to a vending machine, so I gave it some spare change in an attempt to help.

Another sign near me has no grammatical errors; it's simply unnecessary. The cheapest gas in town is just down the street, but the pump traffic is maddening. In a last-ditch effort to maintain order, they put signs up at the respective end of each pump row: "Exit only" and "Enter only." I can understand the first one – someone might be headed toward that row, then see that they're approaching the exit. But when would someone be in danger of breaking an "Enter only" regu-

lation? If they're looking at the sign, they're already entering
– unless they happen to read it in their rearview mirror, in
which case it's already too late.

But I see my word limit is rapidly approaching. This is a
sign I should...obey...and bring my word's to an "end."

- March 2008

A Million Little Pages

To be a book-collector is to combine the worst characteristics of
a dope fiend with those of a miser.

– Robertson Davies

I wake to the drone of my own snores and the feeling of drool dripping down my chin. I open my eyes and I'm on the couch, in the middle of a book. Literally. I must have passed out while reading and had it fall onto my face again.

I look at the clock and see there's no time for a shower. That's okay, I've gone to work reeking of ink before. I think back to the first time...

It's summer 2000. I'm strolling through a mall with my wife, unaware that we are about to walk right into the dealer who will start us on our seven-year addiction.

We round a corner and see the dealer looking open, inviting and warm – not dangerous at all. But books can be deceiving.

I look at the display in the dealer's window, where the four artistically arranged titles draw me in. I turn to my wife and say, "I've heard some buzz about that Harry Potter series; wanna buy some?" No thunderclap follows this question, although it should.

We buy the first two, planning to read them over the summer. Two days later, I go back for the second two. I tell myself it will be comforting just to know they're on our shelves, that I don't really have to read them yet.

That night, I embark on my first all-night reading binge – Azkaban. By week's end, I'm bringing the fourth title to work, hiding it in my car and sneaking out every hour for a quick paragraph just to tide me over.

Once I'm done, I need more. I have too many questions. I return to my dealer for the fifth book. When I learn it hasn't been published yet, I panic. The Query rises in me and I cannot control it. I want that fifth, I scream, give me my fifth!

They sic a manager on me and I'm banned from that Waldenbooks. That's okay; dealers are a dime a dozen here.

It turns out I have plenty of time to find a new one, as it will be three years before the fifth title is published. I turn to other forms of the first four – audiobooks, discussion groups, movies. I even try a fan fiction site for some homegrown. It doesn't abate the need. The Query rises again.

For seven years, I drift through existence, lost in a whirl of theories, dates and meaningless anagrams of characters' names. I fight a losing battle against the Query. I leave four jobs.

We have children. I break the habit for a while. To force myself to be there for them, I imagine them as adults, joining an organization called COPE – Children of Potter Enthusiasts. This works, and I feel shame for the first time.

In July 2007, the British cartel releases the final book. [You might have heard something on the news about this.]

On the release date, the Query rises again. We stock up on non-perishable foods and unplug the phones. We give the kids some Pop-Tarts and let them fend for themselves.

For an entire weekend, there is nothing but the book. Everything else must wait – nutrition, love, basic hygiene.

Between us, we go through 1518 pages in one weekend. And then we go cold turkey.

A week later, running Saturday errands with my kids, I walk into a bookstore and ask the guy if he has any fantasy. He brings me some Tolkien. I thumb through the pages, look at the table of contents, smell the ink. Then I set it down, ask him to reshelve it for me and walk out a free man. The Query is dead.

My son asks if I'm ready to go to the pool. Yes, I'm ready.

————

To the Reader: While recreational book use is not for everyone, it wasn't as bad as I made it sound. It's possible I embellished a little in the name of satire. Just don't tell Oprah; I'd hate for her to Frey me over this.

- August 2007

A Nay for Effort

Period 2:
Geography

I like Geography; I like to know where places are.

— Tom Felton

Treks and Wrecks, Traversing and Cursing

We did not get along together in a five-bedroom house; Dad's idea was to put all of us in a car and drive through the desert at the hottest time of the year. Good call, Dad.

– Bill Hicks

I still remember the wisest thing my father said to me when I was a child. I'd just made a helpful driving suggestion on one of our cross-country vacations when he replied, "You'll have to drive one of these some day, smart guy."

Now that I have, I understand what he was getting at. When a dad is at the end of his rope, he'd probably just as soon use it to bind and gag his young passengers. A day behind the wheel can make any parent feel this way. Anything longer than a grocery run and I'm ready to slam my head in the tailgate. All from dealing with a mere 25 percent of my parents' responsibilities.

Yep, they had eight kids – practically their own ball team. Yet somehow, they never seemed to have a ball….

Each summer, they'd load up our 1971 wood-paneled Plymouth Satellite station wagon (the same model the Brady Bunch drove) with a trunk, ice chest, picnic basket and portable potty, then brave the Interstates with half a dozen backseat drivers. (The age spread among us was wide enough that, fortunately for my parents, the first two were beyond vacationing age by the time the last two came along.)

We'd set out early in the morning, leaving the comfort of our suburban home in Northern Virginia to face grueling, full-tank increments of sitting in the car for 5-6 hours. I'm pretty sure Dad's bladder had a higher capacity than his gas tank.

We had several favorite destinations, alternating between them from one summer to the next – Nags Head, North Carolina; York Beach, Maine; or Estes Park, Colorado. As we covered up to 1700 miles on the road, the kids had opportunities to learn about American geography as well as paternal vocabulary. Dad could let fly with some creative curses, and road trips were sure to stoke his creativity.

I remember tracking curse words the same way we tracked license plates in travel bingo. A common schoolyard vulgarity was nothing more than a Pennsylvania or Florida, but the really choice ones – the phrases introducing us to the little-known middle initials of certain deities, plus other gems – were like Alaskas to our ears.

Sometimes the curses were inspired by our behavior – sabotaging a baloney sandwich with cardboard or holding up a sign to passing cars that said, "Help! I've been kidnapped by polygamists!" Other times it was merely serendipity – a bump in the road prompting a potty spill onto the last of the cookies or a trunk disengaging from the luggage rack (Dad's rope skills knotwithstanding) and going airborne at 70mph somewhere along the great I-80 corridor of the Midwest.

Mom wasn't nearly as entertained by these vocabulary lessons as we were, and went to great lengths to prevent anything that would inspire them. To minimize our bad behavior, she resorted to strict seating plans. Two of us would stretch out in the most coveted niche of the station wagon – what we called "the way back." That location granted a kid several luxuries: full authority over food, beverage and potty disbursement; the ability to look out the tailgate and taunt the drivers unfortunate enough to be stuck behind us (we had yet to learn about road rage); and most importantly, a defensive advantage – those seats were well out of range of the Hand of Dad.

The back seat – a bench that never seemed wide enough, even in our rolling coliseum of a car – held another three. Typically, the youngest was forced to take the middle spot, sacrificing leg room to The Hump. This unwelcome protrusion into the floor of the car was a direct impediment to the comfort of the middle rider, and seemed – to an imaginative young passenger, anyway – to be at least seven feet tall and covered in spikes.

Yet the two outermost siblings had no sympathy for the hump-rider's predicament, refusing to allow any part of him to drift into their space in his quest for comfort. Nope, the hump-rider was expected to bend his knees, prop his feet on top of the hump, and endure. Woe unto him should he fall asleep and allow his head to droop to one side or the other – that was a direct violation of the boundaries, and often resulted in a makeshift sporting event as the other two siblings volleyed the sleeper's head back and forth in an effort to avoid being drooled on.

While the back seat was uncomfortable and often contentious, at least it afforded a small modicum of independence relative to the dreaded final spot. The sixth child – usually the one who'd most recently misbehaved – was stuck in front, right between the authority figures. That way, Mom could keep her eyes (and hands, if necessary) on him and reduce the odds of further cursing from the driver's seat.

That kid had no freedom, but did at least get the full blast of the air conditioning vents. He also got the privilege of working the radio controls, which in retrospect was more of a duty than a privilege.

Radio duty entailed listening for the last garbled Abba lyric to give up the ghost to full-blown static, at which point Dad would admit defeat and concede that yes, we had indeed driven out of range of that particular AM station – something that happened about every 45 minutes or so.

Once we found a new station and approached its broadcast location, the static would gradually become quieter, and six passengers would wait for a few blessed minutes of clarity as we crossed about a five-mile radius around the radio tower, each secretly hoping their favorite song would be the one that happened to be on static-free rotation. It's amazing – not to mention ironic – how three hours of boredom could be alleviated by three minutes of "Seasons in the Sun."

As the oldest of our brood gradually left to start their own families and plan their own trips, our family vacations evolved. AM radio gave way to the Sony Walkman, Dad's bladder became weak enough to stop more frequently, we traded in the wagon for a sedan and the two remaining siblings at home – my younger brother and I – started enjoying the drive a little more.

Yet the worst vacation in our family history occurred during this era. I'll describe it in greater detail in my next column; 'til then, just know that it involved a hurricane, a dead car battery, and Mom's frozen funds. It also resulted in some cursing that was akin to spotting a license plate from Australia.

- July/August 2008

How I Spent My Bummer Vacation

Anyone who says they're not afraid at the time of a hurricane is either a fool or a liar, or a little bit of both.

– Anderson Cooper

My parents faced many challenges vacationing with eight kids over the years, but what finally beat them down was quality, not quantity. The worst vacation occurred with only two of their charges along for the ride – my younger brother and me. We were finally old enough to get along, and the trip to North Carolina's Outer Banks was unexpectedly pleasant. Until Charley showed up.

As hurricanes go, Charley wasn't particularly daunting. He was barely a Category 1, and that for less than a day. But it was enough to bring our vacation to its knees. There was no television in our rented cabin that year, which means two things: we had to talk to each other; and we had no idea that a freak depression had formed just offshore and was moving inland without the usual two weeks' notice.

When we went to Mass that Saturday night, we were surprised to hear people pray that the stalled tropical storm near South Carolina would head back to sea. Afterward, Mom noticed two things about the car – the engine had a hard time cranking and the radio was no longer working. So we bought a transistor radio at a pretty steep price (cash only) from a grizzled old islander who probably wouldn't fear any storm that wasn't raining cinder blocks, and who clearly understood the concepts of supply and demand.

During the night, Charley strengthened to hurricane force and made a beeline for the Outer Banks. The rain had started to fall the next morning as we tossed our luggage in the trunk, jumped into the car and ... tried not to make eye contact with Dad when the engine refused to crank. Cursing was kept to a minimum, though, as it caught on the third or fourth try.

No such luck at the rental office, where Dad discovered three things during his mad dash to the key drop box: the rain was falling much harder now; hurricane force winds can snatch an umbrella right out of a grown man's hands; and our battery was not retaining its charge. He plunged back into the driver's seat just as the car stalled. We were in a deserted lot between Croatan Highway and Virginia Dare Trail, where passers-by were bound to miss us. I'm guessing the sound of Dad's resultant cursing was the only thing that caught the attention of the good samaritan who stopped to charge our battery.

As we pulled out of the lot into stopped traffic, it became obvious that our family was most certainly *not* the first in flight. We were in for a long, slow crossing of Currituck Sound, with a battery that was steadily losing its charge – unless we could avoid using anything that would drain it further. Namely, headlights. So out they went as we crawled toward that bridge. That confounded bridge...

Before that day, I'd never feared bridges. Today, I white-knuckle the upholstery if I even see one (much to the delight of my in-laws, who live near Sunset Beach, North Carolina and look for any excuse to get me onto their one-lane pontoon bridge that bobs on the water like a loose cork).

It's called "gephyrophobia," and like Indiana Jones' fear of snakes, all it took was one unfortunate incident. Wright Memorial Bridge is only three miles long, but it took us five hours to cross it that day. Five hours in the open, buffeted by wind and rain, with nowhere to escape to. I was convinced we were headed for Davy Jones' locker.

We were halfway to the mainland when an unidentifiable indicator light came on. It looked like a hieroglyph, but could just as easily have been a gear, a puzzle piece or a reindeer. Mom rifled through the owner's manual until she found the icon with an explanation. "Your Computer Command Control Center may be malfunctioning," it said. "Consult your dealer immediately."

Stuck on that bridge, years before we'd ever heard of cell phones, we had no hope of contacting a dealer. All we could do was wonder what a Computer Command Control Center is, and hope the indicator light would turn off before it drained the battery's small remaining charge.

But the battery held and we made land, proceeding without headlights up a series of winding, two-lane highways in a storm-induced dusk. We reached Petersburg, Virginia before it became too dark to see. We found a garage about two miles off the exit, where the mechanic said he could fix our problem within five minutes – if only he had the parts. I think he needed a battery, an alternator and a reindeer harness. He kept none in stock, but assured us he could have them at the shop by 10am.

We reminded him we had no place to stay and no way to get there, when he pointed across the street at something vaguely resembling a motel. I'd mistaken it for an abandoned building. We grabbed a suitcase, crossed the highway between police chases and entered the Twilight Zone.

To call that motel "ramshackle" would be insulting to rams. The screen door came off in my hand as we entered the lobby, where the owner was startled to see actual customers. I think he thought we were there to rob him. We paid for our room and asked him if the hotel had a restaurant. He grunted and pointed to a vending machine in the corner. This place wasn't five stars; it was a black hole.

Our room had one source of light – a bare bulb in a shadeless lamp. But it was enough to illuminate the graffiti over the bed – dirty limericks and a phone number. I would have called it for a laugh, but the phone was dead. The bathroom had a shower curtain ... for a door. The shower had nothing. We found one lonely pink towel, but were sure it had once been white.

I wanted to save our dinner leftovers – a couple of generic colas – but when I opened the mini-fridge, there was no sign of cold air. Mom was glad of this, as she was afraid we'd get robbed in the night and she felt a defunct fridge was the perfect place to hide her purse. It must have kicked on during the night, though (maybe the owner remembered to flip the breaker for our room) because the next morning, she was shocked to find her purse covered in frost.

After another death-defying run across the Petersburg Autobahn, we paid for the repairs in cold cash (literally) and enjoyed the quizzical look on the mechanic's face when Mom placed it in his hand. Dad cranked the engine on the first try, we cheered and we were on our way home, each knowing this vacation would be the stuff of legend before day's end.

That was the last time I traveled with my parents, as I graduated and moved out two years later. We've been to the Outer Banks since then, but always coming from different directions in separate cars. And every time I go, I look for a souvenir tee-shirt that says, "My parents went to the beach, and all I got was this lousy gephyrophobia...."

- September/October 2008

Walt Disney, Whirled

No one needs a vacation so much as the person
who has just had one.
– Elbert Hubbard

Today is my wife's birthday. Although it's been 13 months since I announced her age on national television, I'm still making up for it. Not for her sake, as she didn't really seem that upset about it – she just rolled her eyes and shook her head in mock disbelief. I've caught harsher guilt trips for passing gas at family gatherings, something she ought to be used to by now.

Nope, I had to make it up more to other people, the third parties who were shocked that a husband could be so stupid. I tried telling them it wasn't stupidity, it was planned – but that hasn't worked. They still had to be placated, so for all those who thought I'm only a slightly better husband than Ike Turner, Bill Clinton or anyone with the last name Peterson, I took my wife to Disney World last week for an early birthday present.

That's not a big departure for us; in fact, it could be commonplace enough to her that it doesn't make up for the age-dropping. Really, Disney World is a permanent fixture (or fix, as the case may be) in our life. We've come to know it as our place. We honeymooned there and have gone back at least once every year since. We bought property there, and one of the reasons we had kids was to have an excuse to go back more often.

What's more, there are others like us. But we're considered strange. Frequent visits to Disney World are more shocking to third parties than the aforementioned age revelation. An associate once called me a "freak" when he heard how often I go to Disney World; you'd think I'd told him I like to pee on kittens or something. People ask us why we go there so often; I like to respond, "To get away from people who ask us to justify our lifestyle to them." As an added bonus to that, we have more gas money for the trip now that we don't spend it on socializing....

Face it – we like Disney World. But even its biggest fans can admit the place has its negative points – namely, the other people there. As my wife pointed out last week, if it's your first time out of your house, you should try someplace less taxing than Disney World. Because it seems like that's all we see down there – the people my dad used to call "rubes." You know who I mean – the morons without a clue as to how to use a turnstile, stand in line or pay for lunch.

It just feels as if there's an inordinate number of people out there whose sole mission is to tick us off; our only defense against them is the "eighth dwarf" title – a nickname we secretly award to whoever happens to be ruining our fun at the time. An imbecile or otherwise offensive person is much more bearable if we've assigned them an official dwarf name in our minds. While Snow White has her entourage – Happy, Grumpy, Sleepy, Sneezy, Dopey, Doc and Bashful – she generally eschews the ones we've encountered:

Dorky. This was the one that started them all. He's one of those legends that's become so embellished, I can no longer remember the truth. All I know is, he was dressed funny and he did something obnoxious in our proximity, whereupon my wife turned to me and said, sotto voce, "Ladies and Gentlemen...Dorky, the eighth dwarf!" Once I got the joke, I was only too happy to reciprocate and drive it into the ground, relentlessly searching for more eighth dwarves ever since.

Busy. This dwarf doesn't have time for vacation, as his office back home is experiencing all sorts of catastrophes that can't possibly be solved without his involvement. So he's loudly barking orders into the blue tooth that's been glued to his ear, and that's way too close to your ear for you to avoid overhearing. Meanwhile, the children he's ignoring are lashing out in desperate attempts to get someone – anyone – to discipline them. But they could be worse off; they could be the kids of...

Forceful. The aggressive dad, the one you just know is the terror of his kids' soccer coaches back home. He insists that his kids should experience every ride whether they want to or not, because he paid for them, dammit. Also, he rode these coasters when he was their age and it didn't kill him, so if they know what's good for them, they'll shut up and start having a good time, by God.

Dressy. The genius we see at least once in every park — the woman dressed to the nines, as if she's headed to the Oscars instead of the Mickeys. Good call, Lady — it's 100 jillion degrees out, but you look good in fur. And those four-inch stilettos will be even more fun after the first mile, when you realize you're not even halfway around Epcot yet.

Frumpy. Dressy's ugly stepsister. Come on, Grandma, the canary yellow stretch pants are hurting my eyes. And tell your surly high-schooler to save his fishnet jersey for football practice; this park has rules against nipple exposure.

Stinky. On second thought, maybe this guy could use the fishnet, to air out a little. While I hate getting stuck next to him on the 20-minute "It's a Small World" boat ride, at least his body odor gives me something to think about before that song drives me out of my mind.

Thrifty. No, you can't order the kids' meal, Sir. Please stop holding up the food line. Here's a clue — you're in a theme park that's essentially on an island in the middle of a swamp, so you can't get back to the parking lot without relying (and waiting) on their official transportation. They have you where they want you, which is at their monopolizing mercy. If you didn't want to pay $17.50 for a Clarabelle Burger, you should have smuggled in some non-perishable items to tide you over.

Pushy. Settle down, friend. The line's stopped moving again, and you're not going to get into a spinning teacup any faster by riding my back pockets. They might not have concepts like patience and personal space in your culture, but in mine, your eagerness has gone past rudeness and entered the realm of marriage proposal. If you don't back off, I'm going to share a little talent with you that my wife hates for me to show off at family gatherings. Which leads me to...

Gassy. Doesn't matter which line you find yourself in; this dwarf will be in it. He enjoys dropping a little stealth bomb while ostensibly chatting up his linemate, making you wish under your fiercely held breath that he'd go chat up Doc, instead.

Kvetchy. It's too hot. It's too cold. If we were back in East Orange, they'd be able to handle these crowds. This dwarf doesn't mind telling you how much better things are at home, and all you can think of is how much you wish they were there right this minute. Often seen with...

Whiny. Pretty much every kid there who's not one of ours.

Trampy. (Not to be confused with Tramp, an actual character and one of the lovable furheads whose autograph your kids will want.) Put a tee-shirt on, Lady! No one wants to see your tattoos. Displays like that are the reason we don't take our kids into the "Wonders of Life" pavilion....

Wheely. Rockin' the electric cart to the point of reckless endangerment. Slow down there, Easy Rider. They rent those things for transportation, not crowd disbursement. Besides, I'm not convinced you need it. Laziness isn't really a disability, you know. I know you can walk just fine; I saw you make a break for the Jungle Cruise when you thought you were going to get stuck behind that Brazilian tour group.

Baleful. No, thank you, I don't want a punch in the mouth. It was nice of you to offer, though, and I'm sure your wife and kids are duly impressed with your heroic antics. I've learned a valuable lesson, so the next time you push my kid down while you're running for the front car of the Monorail, I'll be sure to remember my place and hold my tongue. By the way, see that security camera over there? The guys on the viewing end have probably already dispatched a security team to welcome you at the next stop. Enjoy your ride!

Sadly, I've run into all of these dwarves on one trip or another. Is it any wonder we consider Disney World the happiest place on Earth?

- February 2008

This Kid Could Go Far (If Only He Could Drive)

Grown-ups never understand anything for themselves, and it is tiresome for children to be always and forever explaining things to them.

– Antoine de Saint-Exupery

O ur son recently had his sixth birthday; we gave him a road atlas. Before you condemn us as poor gift-givers or parents who can't relate to our kids, dig this – it was his favorite gift. He really wanted a new one, as his old copy was falling apart.

This was the day before Father's Day, so after giving my child an atlas, I got my gift – Diddy Kong Racing. It plays on my Nintendo DS, which he gave me for Father's Day last year – two days after receiving a calculator for his birthday. Freaky Friday, anyone?

The birthday boy – let's call him "Doodlebug" – loved the atlas. A deluxe edition, it's vastly superior to the old one.

"Words fail!" he exclaimed after unwrapping it. We think that means Doodlebug is pleased.

The deluxe version is spiral-bound with heavy pages, coated for easy cleaning. (You never know when a childish person might play with your atlas and get it dirty.) Doodlebug appreciates the added protection against the possibly dirty hands of his irresponsible two-year-old brother, Sugarbear.

Of course, the new atlas retains all the features he liked in the old one – mileage tables, alphanumeric grids and population listings. Plus, it includes Canada and Mexico – a must for any would-be traveler of North America.

Not that Doodlebug is a big traveler; he's been in only ten percent of the United States. He has grandparents in Virginia, so we go there occasionally. He has grandrodents in Disney World, so we go there frequently. Those drives account for four additional states; toss in his native stomping grounds and he's been in five. He's obsessed with the other 45 (also D.C. and Puerto Rico).

Doodlebug was disappointed about one thing – we didn't think to give him a ruler, for computing distances between cities. He's tired of borrowing mine, which with mere eighth-inch increments doesn't yield nearly the level of precision he requires.

He feels compelled to track nationwide distances, so he painstakingly records them in tables. Color-coded for metric and standard. In Microsoft Excel. Honest to God.

We were grocery shopping a week before his birthday and I asked him if he wanted to stop and order a cake on the way home. His reply? "No thanks, I have to get home soon; I have some work to do."

"What work? You're five!"

"Daddy! I haven't finished my spreadsheet of distances from Raleigh to major cities in Montana!"

"And this is for...?"

"When we go there one day."

"Why would we go to Montana, Doodlebug?"

"Because we've never been!"

"We've never been to Siberia, either, but that doesn't mean we should go."

"Don't be silly, Daddy – we can't drive to Siberia."

"I'm not even sure we can drive to Montana – I wouldn't know how to get there."

"That's easy – go from North Carolina through Tennessee, Kentucky, Illinois, Iowa and South Dakota, and you're there!"

I ran the cart into a Mrs. Paul's display in shock. After regaining some composure and the use of my shins, I checked his hands for crib notes. None – he was mapping from memory. I quizzed him on a longer trip; he nailed it. I gave him a coast-to-coaster; no problem. I invented a state; he wasn't fooled.

I felt like Charlie Babbitt quizzing Rainman on which cards were left in the blackjack decks, secretly scheming to turn a profit from the abnormalities of his own flesh and blood. For one sick moment, I felt guilty about it. Fortunately, that moment passed.

We sped home so Doodlebug could finish his spreadsheet before I gave him a new assignment to complete on his computer. He's now Googling kids' game shows whose top prizes could pay off two mortgages, an SUV and three credit cards, with enough change to afford a Montana vacation.

I'd research it myself, but his computer's better. Plus, I've been busy racing Diddy Kong.

- July 2007

A Nay for Effort

Period 3:
Chemistry

Love is the drug I'm thinking of.
            - Bryan Ferry

Romance by Any Other Name

Fifty percent of America's population spends less than ten dollars a month on romance. You know what we call these people? Men.

– Jay Leno

Don't blame me. I wanted to write about a guy topic, but was voted down by the flock of women holding the definite majority at our last editorial meeting (I think Matt might have abstained from voting, but I know he had my back). The ladies seemed to think it would be fun to read my take on Valentine's Day. I tried to warn them, but they insisted.

They went on to discuss the merits of a series of Valentine stories from the other regular writers. One of them suggested a helpful article for guys on a tight budget, suggesting decent Valentine's Day gifts for less than $100. I had to stop them to ask if people actually spend *more* than $100 on Valentine's Day gifts. All I got in reply was several pairs of rolling eyes and the giggling verdict of, "I feel sorry for his wife."

My wife is fine, thank you. She doesn't suffer on account of my lack of Valentine's Day enthusiasm; rather, she shares it. We simply prefer to express our love *every* day of the year instead of just one.

See, I don't have a problem with love. It's the romance part that irks me. I believe romance has been overly, umm, romanticized. Nothing illustrates my point better than the very story that forever linked St. Valentine with the concept of love....

During the third century, Roman Emperor Claudius II felt that soldiers shouldn't be married, lest their longing for wife and home distract them from what he felt should be their true devotion – the duties of war. So he decreed that soldiers remain bachelors. But St. Valentine defied him, wedding soldiers in secret.

So great was Claudius' rage that he developed a facial tic, which was prone to manifest itself at the mere mention of Valentine's name. Wishing to hide their marital status, the soldiers pretended to share their emperor's disdain for Valentine, often imitating his tic in a show of solidarity. This came to be known as the "Roman tic" and in time, any young man who married against the wishes of authority was called a "romantic."

Sound plausible? It's not. In fact, it's a complete fabrication. I apologize and promise not to do that again, but in my defense, I had a reason for lying – I wanted to prove I can be just as romantic as the next guy.

I'm serious – romance is all about lies. If you don't believe me (and I wouldn't blame you if you didn't), ask Noah Webster. I did some research via his online dictionary, and this time my claims are verifiable – feel free to go to **www.webster.com** to check behind me.

Enter "romance" in Webster's search engine and you'll pull up several possible parts of speech. Click on the noun, whose first definition starts out, "a medieval tale based on legend...." Aha! Even Webster's Dictionary admits that romance doesn't exist!

But why settle for one definition? The next one calls romance "something (as an extravagant story or account) that lacks basis in fact." Just as I suspected, romance is nothing more than an extravagant story.

Further evidence comes from the first definition of the intransitive verb form of the word: "to exaggerate or invent detail or incident."

Look up the word "romantic" as an adjective and you'll find definitions such as "having no basis in fact" and "imaginary." Therefore, if you brag that you have a romantic boyfriend, your gal pals are quite accurate to say there's no such thing – if he's romantic, he's imaginary.

I researched this only to prove romance is a sham, but was delighted to find bonus fun in the form of other equally amusing definitions. For example, Webster also says "romantic" means "impractical in conception or plan." No surprise there, really.

But look at definition 5c – "conducive to or suitable for lovemaking." Guys, I want you to remember this the next time a woman calls you "romantic." What she really means is, you're suitable for lovemaking.

Bit of a backhanded compliment, isn't it? When it comes to lovemaking, there's not a man alive who'd be content with being called "suitable." In our minds, that translates to: "Eh. You're sort of okay, I guess. Plus, you don't sweat much for a fat guy." No, thanks.

Ladies, go back to the noun definitions of "romance" for a disturbing surprise at the number 4 spot – it means "love affair." In all caps and hyperlinked, no less. Better think twice before you say you expect more romance from your husband – he might interpret that as, you expect more love affairs from him. Carte blanche.

I think my favorite definition, though, is for "romance" as a transitive verb: "to try to influence or curry favor with especially by lavishing personal attention, gifts or flattery."

That's romance in a nutshell – sycophancy at best, bribery at worst. False all around.

To illustrate the level of sycophancy, I did more research (and this part is true). Consider: the Greeting Card Association estimates that we send *one billion* Valentine's Day cards every year, raising a couple of questions in my mind.

First, why do we have a Greeting Card Association?

Second, how much does this alleged holiday cost? Assuming a very conservative $3 a card, that's at least $3 billion. Now let's further assume half of the cards (500 million, by my count) accompany a gift of some sort – chocolate, jewelry, power tools or that sort of thing.

How much would that cost? Based on our editorial meeting, I'm clearly not the best person to estimate how much one pays for Valentine's Day gifts.

But maybe I'm the only Valentine Grinch, and the aforementioned $100 actually is a decent amount to spend on a gift. Multiply that by 500 million cards and you have another $50 billion being spent in the name of romance. Does this seem wasteful to anyone else?

That's why this year, I'm starting a movement – instead of spending $53 billion on cards and gifts, let's pay down part of the national debt. Who needs romance when you have the Government?

They're pretty similar, anyway – both based on lies, told for the same ultimate goal....

- January/February 2010

Engaged, Outraged, Upstaged

The surest way to hit a woman's heart is to take aim kneeling.
– Douglas William Jerrold

Face it, guys – as a gender, we're skeptical about marriage. I'm not sure why, because it's a wonderful institution. And I should know; I had myself committed to said institution 17 years ago.

But before the bliss comes the blitz – three to eighteen months of panic, otherwise known as being engaged.

You'll fight constantly over insignificant details. Think of it as trial by ire. It starts with the diamond, the perfect analogy for marriage – precious, unbreakable and formed only after a long period of intense pressure.

Buying the ring is your most important responsibility. In fact, it's your only responsibility, so man up and accept it. Letting her choose her ring is akin to admitting you'll never be able to please her – a fact that should take you many more years to accept.

Diamond size is measured in "points" so women can keep score. Nobody would ever say, "Beautiful gown; what's the size?" but it's perfectly acceptable to ask how big of a rock you bought.

They say a ring should cost two months' salary. This is a myth perpetuated only by the people who *sell* diamonds and the people who *wear* them. Be strong; don't let her be as shallow as the stone you want to give her. Practice this line: "It's petite and beautiful, just like you."

Beyond the ring, she gets her way. Be there for planning, but stay out of the way. When she asks your opinion, she only wants you to validate hers. Under no circumstances should you offer an actual opinion. You must pretend to care enough to consider the question, but ultimately agree with her.

There's a look for times like this – when she asks what you think, use it. Imagine you're watching the big game on a television just past her shoulder. Watch intently, as if it's showing a slow-motion replay, then visualize the call going your way. Look at her and say, "Yes! It's good!"

Religion is another area where compromise is essential. If you were raised in different faiths, you'll need to find a denomination that suits you both. Also, it should have a church nearby that's photogenic enough for her wedding album.

We chose Episcopalianism, an effective mix of our religious backgrounds. One night we invited the priest to dinner after pre-marital counseling, and he ordered a beer with his chili. My fiancee had been raised Baptist, so she was shocked to see a minister drinking. I'd been raised Catholic, so I was shocked to see him stop at only one. We adapted eventually.

Some couples write their vows. If she hasn't heard of this, keep it to yourself! But if she wants to try it, go along with the concept. Just don't attempt to write your half, especially if you want to avoid offending her, her parents, the officiant and the guests. Instead, shell out the money to have it secretly written by a freelancer. Trust me. I'm a freelancer.

You'll be expected to attend bridal shows. Wear a nice shirt, practice your smile and hold your complaints for the six-hour duration. Or just move to where her maid of honor lives, so she can take your place at these events. It's worth the expense.

You can also buy bridal magazines for ideas. There are several that, inexplicably, publish new issues monthly. Each looks like the previous; buy it anyway. She knows the difference and wants them all. If you're engaged less than a year, maybe you won't have to subscribe.

She'll grow her hair out, which you'll like. Don't get used to it. She'll butcher it within months, as it's for photos only – kinda like Glamour Shots.

Remember favor bags at birthday parties when you were a kid? Some couples give them at weddings. Seriously. If she suggests this, don't laugh – it's not a joke.

Bridal showers are no longer for women only. If you get invited to a "couples shower," don't get too excited – it's not nearly as fun as the name implies.

There will be other minor details such as invitations, flowers and the reception. You don't pay for those, so just mimic her mother's opinions. The two of them agree on everything, anyway. Don't they?

If you think you might be getting cold feet, don't fret. There's a simple test to determine whether you're right for each other – if you get through the engagement without killing each other, you are.

Trust me. I'm a freelancer.

- January/February 2010

Love for Sale

You can't put a price tag on love, but you can on all its accessories.
— Melanie Clark

With the holidays immediately past and my heart freshly purged of kindness, January is usually the time I'm at my most cynical. It's also the time I try to set aside to reflect on the people and events from the past year that really ticked me off.

But I'm switching things up this year. I'm saving my angry list for February and addressing that month's frequent topic — love — this month. Except I'm not sure I can do that topic justice. I don't even understand it. Does anyone?

Advertisers don't — love is probably the most overcommercialized, yet misunderstood, commodity in today's market. Consider the two consecutive billboards I noticed on a North Raleigh thoroughfare, each attempting to capitalize on some aspect of love. The first was for a jeweler, the second for a purveyor of more risqué adornments.

The jeweler's ad depicted a woman in full repose, holding her arm over her head to admire her new watch while arching her back in a provocative stance. The watch was the only thing she was wearing, other than a "come hither" grin.

Her look was that of a woman about to do something naughty, and the underlying message of the ad was disturbingly clear — "Hey, guy! Give your lady our jewelry, and you, too, could earn some quid-pro-quo lovin'!" It conveyed an unsavory image of both love and commerce, reminding me of the punch line from an old dirty joke: "No, honey — that's where *jewelry* comes from."

The second billboard depicted a more prudish model who was hawking, ahem, *less* prudish items. She was fully clothed and surprisingly vertical. Her smile was worthy of a dentist's billboard — happy rather than devilish. It conveyed unadulterated joy (more like the smile of *man* about to do something naughty).

Either the ads had switched photos, or I misunderstood the products listed on the second one – "novelties and party gifts." Perhaps a "novelty" was nothing more than a whoopee cushion, and "party gifts" could be the Disney baubles I typically buy for my kids' favor bags.

Curious about this, I stopped by the second establishment to conduct some innocent research. Turns out, that was the *only* innocent thing inside that store....

I was greeted by a friendly young clerk named Crystal, who smelled nice and wasn't shy about her impressive measurements. I figured I shouldn't bother asking to see her whoopee cushions, and the baubles displayed in her store were vastly different from the birthday favors I'd bought in the past.

Nor was there a Disney character to be found, even though the store carried an extensive collection of movies. I left with empty hands and red face, thinking Madison Avenue has no business involving themselves in affairs of the heart.

In this age when the average NFL player's contract is longer than the average marriage, I believe we need to reclaim love from the advertisers – it's as foreign to them as truth is to politicians.

Which is why I'm proud that as I write, I'm approaching a marital milestone (not to be confused with a marital millstone). At publication time, I will have just celebrated my 15th anniversary with the woman previously designated here as "Sweetie."

The two types of gifts suggested for the 15th wedding anniversary are, ironically, watches and crystal. Wanting to steer away from both, I opted for a Disney bauble.

It's a little statue that probably looks stupid to anyone else but means something to us. It represents the way our 15 years started and the way they've progressed. She'll probably like it better than she'd have liked a watch, anyway. And I know she'll like it better than she'd have liked Crystal.

Happy anniversary, Sweetie. I love you. It's been a wonderful 15 years, and I hope you'll extend my contract. Sometimes it's been you and me against the world, lately it's been you and me against the kids, and too often it's been you and me against each other. But it's always been you and me re-gardless, and I wouldn't change a thing.

Except maybe to buy you more jewelry.

- January 2008

The Moral Affront of Co-Ed Showers

What is your hosts' purpose in having a party? Surely not for you to enjoy yourself; if that were their sole purpose, they'd have simply sent champagne and women over to your place by taxi.

– P.J. O'Rourke

Modern men face a peril that didn't exist 20 years ago: couples showers. How did this happen? In the glory days, whenever a shower was planned, anyone with a "Y" chromosome had to vacate the premises in advance and avoid coming within 100 yards during the event's duration.

Someone apparently thought our feelings were hurt by the exclusion – she obviously didn't know how much fun we were having behind her back – and we're officially "allowed" to attend now.

Gee. Thanks.

I remember pondering this unseemly trend with the other guys at our baby shower, sitting in the co-host's den and staring forlornly at his unplugged television while we listened to the women talk about Pitocin, Braxton Hicks and other foreign singers.

The Hostess served cake and reminded us that a random slice had a little plastic baby inside. Apparently, whoever gets the baby slice is said to be the next expectant parent!

After applying the Heimlich Maneuver to Willard Kendall, we congratulated him on his upcoming fecundity and proceeded to the games portion of the shower. First up was something with a diaper and a pin. Then a word association game, I think – I wasn't really listening. Lastly, a baby-themed Mad Lib reprinted from a barely legible PDF.

The Mad Lib was mildly entertaining, but only thanks to the co-host's inventive use of obscenities for each noun that he filled in. The guys appreciated the humor; the Hostess did not. Odds were good they would *not* become the next expectant couple.

Salvation arrived via Ronny Slocombe's beer-stuffed cooler. The Hostess was annoyed. Apparently, she intended there to be no alcohol at this party – out of empathy, solidarity or something like that for my wife's mandatory temperance.

Only somebody forgot to tell Ronny. Or maybe Ronny resorted to that ages-old trick known to every guy – pretending to have not heard. What wife could doubt that?

However he did it, Ronny saved the day. The sound of pop-tops on the back porch was invigorating, like a 21-gun salute to our restored masculinity. (If not restored, then at least temporarily on loan by the distaff ones inside.)

We drank, laughed and grunted for a few minutes. I told them the worst thing about pregnancy is the six weeks of celibacy after it's over. They laughed until my wife's voice drifted out of the heretofore unnoticed open window: "Ten, if you're lucky." The guys bowed their heads in a show of sympathy.

Then we proceeded to the moment I'd been dreading – the unwrapping. Men should not participate in this. There should be a law – any man receiving a gift must unwrap it alone, in the sanctity of his own easy chair. Preferably in the dark. Within a few days, maybe his wife can help him write a thank-you note, because God knows we can't come up with them on our own.

A man could write, "Thanks for the bowls" on an index card and be done with it, whereas a woman can fill two sheets of flowery stationery with gratitude, praise and a treatise on the possible display iterations and alternative uses for the bowls. But they're just bowls. Little, colored, plastic bowls that a child is going to slobber on.

Because that's how we see things, we don't know how to open gifts. We can't react properly. Women fawn. Men grunt. If you listen carefully, you might hear a "thanks" within that grunt.

The first gift was some article of baby clothing; I believe my wife called it a "1-Z." That must be a size code or something.

She held it up and asked me if I didn't think it's the cutest thing ever. Unfortunately, it was covered with bugs, so I didn't understand how she thought so. Granted, the bugs were pink and blue with embroidered smiley faces, but they were still bugs – something that elicits shrieks in real life in the bathroom or the kitchen, but is apparently adorable when depicted in the nursery. When I mentioned this out loud, she gave me a look that said grunting would be preferable, and that we were perhaps up to fourteen weeks of celibacy.

Next, a set of bottles – complete with a sponge and something called a nipple brush, which looked a little coarse to me. I warned my wife that it could be painful in her sensitive condition. The guys gave me the laughs I was looking for; she gave me the same disgusted look. I decided to grunt from there on and we got through the rest of the gifts without incident.

As we were leaving, someone asked what we're hoping for. I tell them a girl. Why? Because a boy will grow into a man, a man will grow into a husband and a husband will grow into a father-to-be who will be forced to endure a baby shower.

The look on my wife's face led me to think I shouldn't have made that joke in front of the Hostess. I suspected my wife was now very mad at me. After the door closed, my suspicions were confirmed. She uttered one word: "Eighteen."

Huh?

"Weeks of celibacy! Eighteen. And counting."

Then she said what she thought was the coup de grace, and I had to act disappointed: "That's the last time I bring you to one of these."

Worth every week....

- January 2006

44

A Nay for Effort

Period 4:
Biology

Parents are the last people on earth
who ought to have children.

– Samuel Butler

Foul Line

If nature had arranged that husbands and wives should
have children alternatively, there would never
be more than three in a family.

– Lawrence Housman

In October 2000, when we had yet to provide my parents
with grandchildren, we sent them a Grandparents' Day
card with this note: "Sorry this card is a month late, but
so is your daughter-in-law...."

By that time, we were able to joke about our news. A
week prior, it had been a different story. We made our little
discovery amid more serious matters, like a job change for her
and the World Series for me.

I remember that night as if I'm still living it:

Ready to watch Game One, I bop into the bedroom, looking for my remote. I peek into the master bathroom – just in
case I took it to bed with me the night before – and notice my
wife sitting on the floor in shock. She's clutching what ap-
pears to be a Popsicle stick with two pink lines across it.

"Hey, where'd you find a Popsi–"

"I think it's positive."

"Positive? The Popsicle? What do you–" I stop cold when I
register what she's actually holding.

After a pregnant silence, I grin and move in to hug the
new mother-to-be, who breaks into tears. This confuses me.
It's not good for me to be confused; I usually say stupid
things. That trend continues tonight.

"How are we gonna have a baby?" she gasps between
sobs.

"Well, there are doctors, and–"

"NO! How are we gonna take care of one? We're not
ready!"

"Don't worry; you have eight months to get ready!" (Strike
one.)

46

"Look, would you just confirm this for me?" She stands and holds the stick toward me. I think she wants me to take it.

"Umm...you peed on that, didn't you?"

"Just look at it! It might not be positive. The first line looks a little faint, doesn't it?"

I peek at it from a safe distance. "Yes, but that's the control line – it's permanent. See the really dark line next to it? The one there's no mistaking? The one that couldn't possibly be a smudge? The one that..."

"Okay, I get it!" She plops to the floor again as she flings the stick toward our bathroom counter. I watch it arc in slow motion, land on the counter and take a double bounce before skidding to a stop mere millimeters from my toothbrush.

Seeing my resulting grimace, my wife sobs even harder. "I knew it! You're upset, too!"

"Wha – no, that's not it! I'm just worried about the pee!" (Strike two.)

"Forget about the pee for a minute, would you?!"

"Okay," I vow while shuffling toward the counter. I pretend to lean against it in a sensitive listening pose, surreptitiously grabbing a couple of tissues. When I make a move for the stick, she screams, "Don't you dare pick that up! Are you even paying attention to me?"

"Sure; how else would I have known where you threw it?" More sobs. "Sweetheart, what's wrong? Aren't you happy?"

"Of course I'm happy! But I'm scared, too! I'm starting a new job next week; what will my boss say when I show up on the first day and tell her oh, by the way, in eight months, I'm taking maternity leave?"

"She'll probably say, 'Okay, let me start the paperwork.' You know how long HR takes with these things."

She stops crying long enough to glare at me.

"Sweetie, listen." I plop down next to her, give her a reassuring hug and continue holding her, the smartest thing I've done all night. "There's nothing wrong with being pregnant at a new job. There's nothing wrong with being pregnant, period. Believe me, she won't think poorly of you."

The sobbing slows as she looks up at me. "Really?"

"Really," I reassure her as I wipe a tear away. She almost grins. I'm doing well. I could stop talking now. Unfortunately, I don't.

"What will make her think poorly of you is if you start blubbering like this on your first day of work." (Strike three! He's outta there!)

She stands and walks out of the bathroom in silence.

I tell myself I've already helped in some small way – after all, she's no longer scared or sad. Instead, she's back to a state more familiar to her after eight years of marriage to me – raging disgust.

When I enter the bedroom, I see my lost remote in plain sight and almost dance with joy. I grab it and point it at the TV, then turn my eyes on the door to the hallway – where my newly pregnant wife has just left in confusion, fear and scorn. Should I go after her, maybe try again?

I look back at the TV.

Back at the hallway.

TV.

Hallway.

I decide.

Looks like tonight's game has been called....

- October 2007

Poker Face

*Most of us become parents long before
we have stopped being children.*

– Mignon McLaughlin

Every dad has an inner guy – the voice of his former loutish self, now allegedly tamed in the name of marriage and parenthood. Mine is named Cretin. I hide him from my sons and only occasionally reveal him to my wife.

To that end, I use a tool that's freely available to anyone who needs it – the poker face. Mine helps me bluff against Cretin's true feelings and hides my lack of conviction in whatever I'm outwardly saying, such as "Sure, I'd love for your parents to come and stay with us for a week" or "That's okay, I wasn't interested in the game, anyway – I'd much rather help you fold laundry."

It also helps prevent my sons from acting like I once did. Whenever I try to teach them a moral lesson, no matter how unconvinced Cretin is of its rightness, I wear my poker face and hope the boys buy it. Sometimes it works; this story isn't about one of those times.

On the night in question, my three-year-old had asked me to keep him company while he used the potty. If that sounds weird, you probably don't have kids who are toilet-trained. There comes a time during the early stages when they decide they just don't want to be alone in there. The boys will one day learn to think of that room as their sanctuary, but until then, it's a parent's obligation to stand in there with them and be subjected to whatever thoughts cross their minds.

So there I was, leaning against the sink and lost in my own meaningless thoughts, until he cut the proverbial deck and forced me to break out my poker face. At first he was just sitting there, seeming to stare down into the toilet. Without warning, however, he reached between his legs, took hold of himself "down there" and examined said area for a good minute or two. The cards were being dealt.

Before we go any further, I must relate my family's code word for the male genitalia. This worries me. I'm sure all families have code words, but I'm embarrassed to share mine – I know that's a contradiction when you consider that they're supposed to be euphemisms, but I'm still embarrassed.

I suppose they're like those cute little pet names we reserve for our spouses' ears only. I don't want the guys at work to hear me call my wife "Sweetie" and I don't want them to know what I call my other beloved.

At any rate, we give them nicknames. My parents used one, and when my wife wanted to use one with our son, it seemed only fitting to continue the paternal family tradition. So our codeword is "doodah."

There, I've said it. Let the mockery commence. My family refers to the penis as the "doodah."

This caused some confusion in my youth, as I often wondered what could possibly have inspired the Camptown Ladies to sing that song. I also thought "Zip-a-Dee-Doodah" was about a bathroom visit gone horribly awry.

Anyway, there sat my son, contemplating his doodah. I mean serious, first-time-seeing-a-Dali contemplation. He stretched it out, rotated it and stared unfalteringly for what seemed forever before tucking it in and dubiously asking, "Daddy?"

That question, asked when one has just resolutely considered one's doodah, will never have a satisfactory answer. Any further conversation cannot possibly end well. And on this night, it was tantamount to saying, "Ante up!"

"Yes, son?"

"Deejay's doodah is little."

I wavered only for a moment before biting my tongue to reestablish control of my facial muscles. I also needed that time to remember whom he was talking about; Deejay is a kid from his preschool.

Poker face etched in stone, prepared to defend his classmate against the sadly familiar, belittling gossip of the playground set, I demanded, "Who said that?"

"Nobody said it, it's just...Deejay has a little doodah."

Uh-oh. He wasn't repeating a schoolyard taunt, he was asserting his own extracurricular observation. Of all weeks for his teachers to have started discussing units of measure-ment!

"That doesn't really matter, son."

Sure it doesn't, chided Cretin. *Of course it matters! It matters when you take your first shower in gym class, it matters when your fraternity brothers are assigning nicknames and it matters when you're trolling for bridesmaids at a buddy's wedding. Obviously, it also matters when you share a Montessori bathroom!*

"Don't worry about what Deejay looks like," I continued through my poker face, resolutely ignoring Cretin. "Everyone has differently sized body parts. Take your hands, for instance—"

"But Deejay's doodah is really small."

"That's what I'm trying to tell you. It's okay if—"

"Smaller than mice!"

"Whuh? Well, that doesn't matt—"

"*Baby* mice!"

"It's okay to be sma—"

"Really *little* baby mice!"

Cretin was already trying to answer, *Oh, well, that makes a difference; why didn't you say so? That IS small. Deejay is weak. I'm glad we had this talk, son.*

A more appropriate answer might have been, "Please don't tell Deejay. He'll find out all too soon, anyway."

I said neither. I couldn't speak; I was too busy folding my hand.

Wracked in convulsions that utterly betrayed my poker face, I stumbled into the living room to tell my ace-holding wife that her son had a hand even she might not beat, all the while thinking, *Poor Deejay! I hope he never joins a fraternity....*

- December 2005

Sweat of Beads

A child is a curly, dimpled lunatic.
- Ralph Waldo Emerson

The only thing more traumatic than the first day of school is the first day of camp. Kindergarten offered experienced teachers and an established curriculum; camp offers teenagers and water sports. A little too "Friday the 13th" for my comfort level, but I'm sure my son will be fine if he lasts through lunchtime without incident.

My microwave pizza has 21 seconds left when the phone rings.

"Mr. Bain, your son has a bead stuck up his nose."

"I'm sorry – a bead?"

"For participation and character traits. Some kids put them on a string; yours put it up his nose. It's a standard craft bead – 9mm."

"Like the gun?"

"Just the bullet."

"I feel much better."

"Don't panic; this happens frequently."

"I'll be right there."

I drive like a bullet myself, park in the loading zone and sprint to the counselor's office. She hands me a flashlight and says if I shine it straight up his nostril, I can see the offending bead.

"Which one?" I ask.

"Aquamarine. It's for group swim."

"No, no, no – which nostril?"

"Oh! The right."

I shine, look and see nothing. Having tapped my medical expertise, we head for the pediatrician.

The doctor suggests several drops of antihistamine directly up the nose; my son looks at the dropper and protests that he hates having things like that shoved up his nostril. We revel in the irony for a moment before returning to the task at hand.

My job is to reassure my son while holding him flat on the table with his head dangling off, for easier dropper-to-nostril access. As the doctor advances, my normally docile little boy transforms into an angry, cornered panther. I fall back with scratches down both arms, but the doctor is able to get 2-3 drops on target before taking a claw to the head.

He calls two nurses, a receptionist and a billing clerk to restrain my little werecat while he attempts to retrieve the bead with six-inch tweezers. They never have a chance.

After three aborted nostril forays and an assortment of counter-attacks accompanied by leonine screams, the doctor is happy to recommend a specialist. Once the billing clerk has cleaned her facial lacerations, we settle our co-payment and trek onward.

An hour later, we find the office of the referred plastic surgeon. "Because the bead's plastic?" asks my again-human offspring. I'd chuckle if I weren't in pain.

We explain to the plastic surgeon that my son has a camp bead lodged in his nostril.

"Which one?" he asks.

"The right one."

"No, no, no – which bead? My kids go to that camp."

"Umm, aquamarine?"

"Wow! He did group swim already?"

He locates the bead and reaches for a long, stainless steel suction tube. When my son emits a guttural growl, I ask the doctor if he believes in lycanthropes. He changes his mind and schedules surgery under general anesthesia.

After dinner, we head to the hospital to meet the surgeon, his nurse, an anesthesiologist, a vitals monitor and a med student who wants to observe the procedure. My wife remarks that it took fewer attendants to get our son out of her than it will take to get a bead out of him.

They dope him up with Versed and wheel him away while he's still giggling. Moments later, the surgeon returns with an aquamarine bead in a specimen jar. The procedure took 15 seconds, but the panther wakes slowly over 30 minutes. After he trees the recovery room nurse, we head for our van and civilization.

Back at home, the savage beast is soothed with a plate of mac and cheese, and begins to fill me in on the rest of his day – including the rest of his beads.

"I got the blue one for honesty and the yellow for respect, Daddy."

"How about this green one? What was this for?"

"Responsibility."

"Oh. Well, I'm certainly glad you showed some of that today...."

- September 2007

Sleeping with the Sharks

Oh, the shark has pretty teeth, dear,
And he shows them pearly white.
— Bertolt Brecht

Greetings, readers! My name is Andi Nab; I'm Dan Bain's agent and am submitting this column for him. Dan's regular readers are probably wondering where he is; allow me to explain to both of you.

Dan took his son's Cub Scout pack to Ripley's Aquarium in Myrtle Beach Saturday for an event called, "Sleep With the Sharks®." During the drive home Sunday, Dan passed out on his laptop and has since remained comatose. He was working on the following journal entry:

8pm – The turnstiles open and a blue and gold swell hits the stairs. We reach the private back room and listen to the rules – no running, find a buddy, no caffeine for kids, but de-caf drinks will be available. Good. I'm thirsty from dinner at the pizza buffet.

8:15pm – We embark on self-guided tour; I can't find drinks anywhere.

8:30pm – We enter the 330-foot plexiglass tunnel where we'll eventually sleep. It's narrow and surrounded by sharp-toothed fish. They call it "Dangerous Reef." They expect us to sleep here?

8:45pm – We emerge from the other end of the tunnel to a room devoid of drinks. Doodlebug plays with horseshoe crabs at the touch tank, where the water smells a little too funny to sample. My thirst grows.

9:00pm – We enter the Pirates display. The boys play with cannons while I attempt to pry the lid off a rum barrel.

9:30pm – A ray splashes Doodlebug in the face. I'd call him lucky, but my mouth is too dry to talk.

10:00pm – The aquarium closes and our hosts take us to a classroom for a "learning experience." Some of the boys nod off. Drinks are not provided. I can no longer swallow.

11:00pm – We go to Craft and Snack Time. Snacks include drinks! I drink three gallons of pink lemonade while Doodlebug paints a tee-shirt. When they finish, the boys eat enough cookies to keep them up for another two hours.

Midnight – We set up camp in the tunnel. The lights go out. Doodlebug is nervous about the sharks surrounding us, and talks to me for 90 minutes about grim ways to die. He drifts off around 1:35. I try to sleep, but there's a sawfish leering at me.

2am – Severe cramps hit. Stupid lemonade. I stand up, double over, and am nose-to-snout with a moray eel. I almost scream.

2:30am – I set out in search of the restroom. Several barracudas track me to the end of the tunnel.

2:45am – They are waiting for me when I return, and track me back to my sleeping bag.

3am – I wake up and have to go to the bathroom again. I wish I'd just stayed thirsty last night.

3:30am – I notice a sign claiming the tunnel is strong enough to withstand several hundred elephants. But I realize elephants don't have seven rows of very sharp teeth. I won't sleep again this night.

4am – Two large sand sharks are circling me overhead. I can read their thoughts. "Hey, my favorite! Help me get this container open...."

5am – Am having a staring contest with a leopard shark who's taken a keen interest in my movements. Why won't it blink?

5:30am – Can sharks smell fear?

7am – The boys are up and breakfast is served. More sugar.

8am – We drive to the in-laws' house to meet up with Sweetie and Sugarbear, who spent the night in cushy beds. Sweetie will drive us home after I shower, but I'm afraid of the water. I nap on the couch.

2pm – We're headed home. From the corners of my eyes, I see ghostly silver things floating outside the car. Following us. Watching me. They're trying tooooooooooooooooooooooooo

The journal ended there, when Dan fell nosefirst onto the "o" key. We managed to clean the drool off his keyboard and save the file. We hope he will wake up before press time, but until then, Dan Bain sleeps with the sharks....

- April 2008

A Nay for Effort

Period 5:
Shop/Home Ec

Some people are so busy learning the tricks of the
trade that they never learn the trade.

– Vernon Law

A Derby Job, But Somebody's Gotta Do It

Men have become the tools of their tools.
– Henry David Thoreau

I've been feeling sensitive lately about gender stereotypes and the nicknames that come with them. Why is "soccer mom" the preferred term? How unfair is it that moms get stuck with chauffeur duties based on gender alone?

I have to admit, though, that I might not have cared so much if I hadn't become a "derby dad" this winter.

Our six-year-old Cub Scout – let's call him "Doodlebug" – brought home his first Pinewood Derby kit last December. It's a Cub Scout tradition to race little pinewood cars every year. But when Doodlebug dumped his box on the table, I thought we'd been the victims of a cruel joke. There was no car inside that box!

Instead, there was only a seven-inch block of pinewood, four nails, and four plastic wheels. When I realized the implication, I looked at my wife and said, "Good luck with that." She responded with her "Nice try" smirk.

Seems it's just *assumed* the dad is the right man for this job. But that assumes every dad is a handyman, which I am decidedly not. Although I did replace our kitchen sink last fall. Top to bottom, fixtures to pipes. I'm still proud of that project, but it effectively tapped my life's supply of handiness.

I didn't even have the right tools to make a Pinewood Derby car. At first we tried a coping saw, but apparently we couldn't cope. Having bent its supposedly indestructible, carbon steel blade beyond recognition, I did what any dad would do – I bought a power tool. Unfortunately, there's no storage space in my house for the big ones, and I'm obviously not going to build an addition any time soon. So we settled for the miniature version of a power tool – a $65 handheld rotary tool by Dremel.

60

Some handymen prefer to work with a stationary Dremel, so I bought the $35 vice that's designed especially to hold it still. Because that vice can be clamped to almost any surface, we were able to set up shop in the only room with available space – our kitchen.

I clamped the vice to our table, locked the Dremel in place and took the pine block to it – whereupon it took the pine block from me. Turning at an approximate speed of 35,000 rpm, the blade grabbed the block and catapulted it across the room, where it left a nice scratch on my new sink. Did I tell you I installed that myself?

Reversing the handyman's preferred setup, I clamped the block in the vise and held the tool. This worked better, although the Dremel came close to going airborne a few times.

Once Doodlebug had watched me long enough to know what not to do, he took some turns with the Dremel and we bonded over the shared use of a power tool. He didn't believe me when I tried to tell him the vacuum cleaner is another fun one, so it fell to me to clean up the inch of pine dust from our kitchen floor and table.

After the block had been reduced to what was arguably a car shape, Doodlebug picked a design scheme – black paint with solar system stickers. Painting and finishing progressed without incident (probably because they involved neither power tools nor me) and "The Comet" was born – for only slightly more than our out-of-pocket costs from when Doodlebug was born.

On the night of the race, I realized just how far the Pinewood Derby has come since I was a Cub Scout. Participants take a more professional and/or perfectionist attitude toward it now, immobilizing their cars for transportation in either a metal carrying case or a shoebox with packing peanuts. I looked down at Doodlebug's brown paper bag and mumbled an apology as we walked into the gym.

We passed our pre-race inspection and watched as the judge placed The Comet in the impound area. My jaw dropped as I realized car designs have also changed. My generation chose from making a red car, a yellow car, or a black car. The really creative kids daringly opted for a blue car.

Today's Cubs shape their cars like anything *but* cars; already in impound were cars shaped like coyotes, pencils, coffins, the Black Pearl, tigers, guitars, hot dogs, condiments, skateboards, the Loch Ness monster, R2-D2, penguins and golf courses (complete with players, trees, sand traps and beer carts). Ours looked like...a black car.

Two designs really stood out, the first being a tub of popcorn. That's sort of an inside joke among Cub Scouts; it's akin to a Girl Scout building a car that looks like Thin Mints. The other one is what I've come to refer to as the "Second Amendment Special." It looked like a military humvee, but mounted on its roof was an actual bullet – .308 diameter, 150-grain, flat-base Sierra. Standard sniper round, so I'm told. But it was loaded into an unfired brass, so there was nothing to set the charge off. Therefore, the dad assured me, it would neither harm spectators nor give that car an unfair speed advantage.

The final difference from 30 years ago is in the races themselves. The winners used to be deemed by human judgment, often resulting in disputed calls and occasional fistfights. That actually happened in my hometown. I still can't believe Ryan Wood's dad punched our Cubmaster.

Today's races are monitored by state-of-the-art technology, as metal tracks with sensors in the finish lines determine the winner of each heat. They convey this information to a computer which, if loaded with the proper BSA-approved software, can display the finish times. No disputes, no shiners.

The Comet clocked in at 2.35 seconds from start to finish, which converts to 209.2 mph. Since this was the top time for his den, Doodlebug got to compete at the District level in March. And as the father of one of the winners, I got the prize of being placed on next year's Derby Committee. Which means I get to assemble next year's track.

My wife is still chuckling about that, but she won't be laughing much longer. Doodlebug just signed up for soccer....

- May/June 2008

Wreck the Halls

Never worry about the size of your Christmas tree. In the eyes of children, they are all 30 feet tall.

– Larry Wilde

My family's favorite holiday tradition is the nightly light show, when we hop in the car and drive around random neighborhoods, enjoying other people's decorations. Probably because we can't stand looking at our own.

Try as we might to keep up with the Osbornes, something causes problems with our decorations every year. Specifically, me.

Whenever I touch any complicated electrical item, it begins an almost certain countdown to an early death. I've ruined three iPods, two digital cameras and a laptop over the course of my life, but at least those were cheaper to replace than some of the Christmas decorations I've sent to an early grave.

I'm talking about those big, gawdy things that light up, move, play music and practically bake cookies. We try to display something glitzy in the yard every year, just to draw people's eyes away from the backdrop that is our front porch. It needs all the distraction it can get from its four meager strings of white lights. Plain as can be, they don't even blink. Even though last year, they sent me over the blinking edge....

The Sunday after Thanksgiving, I untangled them for an hour, tested each by plugging it in separately and daisy-chained them in preparation for the Annual Railing Wrap. The chain must be wrapped around the front railing in precise two-inch increments, looped twice around the main column at the top of the stairs and tastefully draped along the railing that descends those stairs.

I did all this, plugged in the end of the chain and went inside to wait for nightfall. When I came back outside to behold my handiwork after dark, one length of the chain was no longer working – oddly enough, only *half* of one of the four strings. Regardless, that string would have to be replaced, so I made a hasty trip to the store for a new one.

Upon returning, I undraped, unlooped (twice) and unwrapped half of the chain, only to realize I couldn't remember which of those two strings had a faulty section. So I plugged them in again – and every light came on. I shrugged, unplugged it, re-wrapped, re-looped (twice) and re-draped it. When I plugged it in, the same length was dark again.

Now I was getting somewhere. Obviously, something about the wrapping, double-looping and/or draping was causing a short. So I proceeded with my original Plan B, which was to simply replace that string with the one I'd just bought. But when I pulled out the new string, I realized it was only half the length of the old one. That's when I treated the neighborhood to a not-so-joyful chorus of words, some of which might have been arguably related to Christmas.

Thoughts cleared by my seasonal invective, I devised a great, Grinchy plan to cheat the system. Although the new string was shorter than the rest, it was the same length as the unlit portion of the old one. I added it to the chain near the shorted end, hiked up the functional part to meet it, tied off the shorted length like a tourniquet and tossed it over the edge of the porch.

Voila! From the street, there appeared to be a seamless transition from one working light to the next. As for the unsightly mass of dead lights dangling behind our hedges, it should only have been obvious to an eavesdropper. Or a fire marshal.

Of course, the end result was still a boring chain of white lights, but we weren't about to alleviate that with yet another train in the yard. See, the previous three years we'd purchased a festive plastic train with chaser lights that looked like billowing smoke and turning wheels. And around the second week of the previous three Decembers, the chasers had stopped chasing, leaving the smoke and wheels illuminated without the illusion of motion.

Which was fine...until the third week. That's when the lights on the wheels and smoke burnt out each year, resulting in the appearance of a mysterious ghost train hovering in mid-air in our yard, apparently powered by clean fuel.

Sell me a faulty Christmas train once, shame on you. Sell me a faulty Christmas train four years running, shame on me. That's why last year, I put my foot down and we refused to buy the same train again. At first I wanted to simply turn on our floodlights, declare them decorative and be done with it. But in an inexplicable fit of Christmas spirit, we eventually opted for one of those popular light-up inflatables.

I pushed this decision against the better judgment of my wife, who feels that inflatables are tacky. I should have listened to her, knowing from observation just how much the inflatable trend had already gotten out of hand – while casing decorations one night the previous Christmas, we'd spotted a house with an inflatable *nativity* out front.

I'm no theologian, but I'm sure there must be some tenet against this. If not, there ought to be. It just seems wrong to turn a solemn religious icon into a goofy light-up balloon. As a rule of thumb, if Macy's isn't willing to denigrate it in their parade, we shouldn't denigrate it in our front yards – they don't fly the Virgin Mary in their city; we should give her the same dignity in our suburbs.

Nativities should be tasteful. Inflatable virgins are not tasteful. Frankly, they tend to draw an unwholesome connotation; I think the last time I saw one was during a bachelor party....

So we went the way of the secular inflatable – a giant snowglobe displaying Santa and an elf standing on either side of a stack of presents, atop which sits a cute little penguin. Unlike the previous three years' worth of trains, the globe lit up and worked fine – for about a week. That's when I suspect Santa sprang a slow leak.

Each night, he'd lean a little further away from the stack of gifts. Maybe he was trying to escape his work, maybe he was simply afraid of the penguin. (Understandable, considering he's not likely to have ever encountered one – the mere presence of a penguin in the North Pole should elicit some suspicion, at the very least.)

By the end of the season, Santa was standing at a 45-degree angle, held up only by the wall of the snowglobe, and looking like a drunk asking for change. I couldn't set him upright again, as he was hermetically sealed inside the globe.

And the further he leaned, the more his waving hand turned into an accusing finger – Santa became my own Tell-Tale Heart, drawing the attention of the rest of the world to the last thing I wanted them to notice. He was pointing right at my hedges, behind which dangled what I'd hoped no one else would ever see – a bizarre clump of dead lights, tied off from the railing like a tourniquet and tossed into the bushes in a fit of laziness.

But that's okay – Santa wasn't the only one drawing attention to the lights behind the holly. Around the third week of December, they inexplicably turned on again – and blinked.

Next year, it's the floodlights for sure....

- November/December 2008

Masking My Contempt

Clothes make a statement. Costumes tell a story.
— Mason Cooley

I'm writing this for the September-October issue during the first week of July, which means two things: it's too hot to think about an autumnal topic, and my editorial process is entirely too long.

But even with more than three months to go, it's not too early for other members of my household to think about Halloween — our boys have already chosen their costumes. And we were stupid enough to buy them this early, which also means two things: they'll change their minds before October, and the costumes will be in shreds by then, anyway. Especially since our three-year-old insists on wearing his every night, "to pactice." Also, to push Daddy to the brink of a coronary...

There I'll be, writing at my computer, oblivious to the little footsteps approaching from behind. I'll turn around to reach for my thesaurus and instead find a 40-inch Darth Vader glaring at me, plastic lightsaber at the ready. While that might not sound formidable in retrospect, trust me — the initial jolt is still pretty unsettling. It makes me long for the old days, when costumes weren't that scary.

I grew up wearing those old "mask and smock" sets by companies like Ben Cooper and Collegeville. They came in a thin cardboard box with a cellophane window on top to display the mask. During good years, I'd get to buy a new set, and would look forward to that magical September day when the seasonal aisle at Drug Fair lost its obnoxiously jeering "Back to School" sign and gained a "Trick or Treat" sign in its place. The shelves were emptied of pencils and spiral-bound theme books, then filled with Ben Cooper boxes — the alleged likenesses of monsters and heroes staring out at me, beckoning with their empty eyes for me to drop $1.99 of my parents' money on one of them.

Yet they were the worst costumes ever. The masks were made of flimsy plastic, prone to bending and tearing, with two weak staples barely holding the elastic "strap" – a cheap, skinny rubber band – in place. If it didn't snap before trick-or-treating was over, that kid had lucked out. I can't remember how many injuries I sustained to various parts of my head and face – if it wasn't a snap to the back of the head, it was hair getting stuck in the staples and pulling out of my head when I removed the mask at the end of the night.

Yet those were better than the other possible injury – the staples tended to come unbent, resulting in sharp metal points extending perpendicularly from the mask's inner surface toward the kid's face. I must have inadvertently pierced my ears a dozen times in my youth. And the razor thin plastic of the masks could deliver precision slices worse than any paper cut I've ever received. It's a good thing I have a big nose, as that kept the danger away from the more sensitive parts of my face.

It was always worth the risk, though, as I felt cooler than the real Fonzie to be dressed as him on Halloween night. I felt like people were convinced that I was actually him, Bugs Bunny, Frankenstein, Evel Knievel or the Six Million Dollar Man – choose your poison. Never mind that the masks didn't actually look like those characters; in my mind, I was their clone.

Besides, if people didn't recognize the character's face, they had the vinyl smocks to clue them in. Those things were even cheaper, with sleeves too short, gaudy color schemes and tie strips attached by a couple of loose threads. Emblazoned across the front, in badly aligned print jobs with the registration marks still showing, was almost always a drawing of the character – along with his/her identity, printed in a prominent location.

So when I rang the doorbell in a cheap Buck Rogers mask, the greeter was able to read my smock, realize whom I was supposed to be, and say something convincing like, "Look, Honey! Buck Rogers is here!" Man, did I think I had them fooled…I never really put it together that Buck Rogers doesn't actually traipse around the 25th century in a tunic bearing his photo and title logo.

Ignorance is bliss, though, and my ignorance kept me blissfully returning to Drug Fair for several weeks in late

September and early October, trying hard to decide between the ten or so characters available that year. If I was lucky, Mom needed to go to the next town over, where Woolworths had twice as many characters waiting to challenge my decision-making abilities.

Some of the lesser-known ones still crack me up when I think about them — what self-respecting kid would go trick-or-treating as Shari Lewis or Mrs. Beasley? And while the Gabe Kaplan might have had a limited appeal, the W.C. Fields was probably the most ill-advised concept ever. ("Here, Danny! Why don't you go as a reputed hater of children, who practically drank himself to death? Trick or treat!") No wonder they were still in stock on All Saints' Day.

But even those poor choices would have been welcomed during the leaner years, when new costume purchases were out of the question. That was when we had to fall back on The Trunk. This artifact sat beneath our basement stairs, collecting dust and mold while it guarded past years' costumes and some old clothes that Good Will had refused to take off our hands. The more imaginative siblings were expected to make costumes from those; I turned to an even less reliable source...

In 1977, the original Star Wars reigned. But the Force wasn't with Ben Cooper, so I decided to *make* a costume from that galaxy far, far away. I wanted to be a Tusken Raider, one of the "Sand People" who'd attacked Luke Skywalker with wicked-looking bludgeons while screaming gutturally under their mysterious facial wrappings. They had cool eyepieces protruding from their heads, which I thought I could duplicate with two empty toilet paper tubes and some Ace Bandages I found at the bottom of my grandmother's closet. I crafted the bludgeon out of a stick and some paper mâché.

The result was laughable, but I did receive kudos at my school's costume parade. I also received a rash on my face for two weeks, thanks to my having neglected to wash the bandages first. (I still think my grandmother must have had a killer combination of weak ankles and athlete's foot.)

Still, it beat the alternative — if we didn't get creative, we'd be stuck wearing The Trunk's old Ben Cooper costumes, complete with flesh-rending tears in the masks and mildew spots on the smocks. Any of us naive enough to wear our siblings' antiquated hand-me-downs would suffer from severe allergies and a head cold for weeks — something to balance out the sick stomachs we got from gorging ourselves on Halloween candy.

But that's another story — while costumes have improved since my youth, treats have taken a turn for the worse. Unfortunately, I don't have enough space left for a proper analysis. Maybe I'll save that topic for next year's autumn issue.

Besides, by the time you read this, I'll already be working on my Valentine's Day piece....

- September/October 2009

Separation Anxiety

The one thing children wear out faster than shoes is parents.
— John J. Plomp

My wife left me today, but I'm not too worried. She'll come back after less than a week, probably on her hands and knees. That's how tired she usually feels after one of her business trips; what did you think I meant?

Anyway, she'll have no right to come home exhausted. Compared to what I suspect I'm about to go through, she's on a five-day vacation. I'll try to blog a daily update to show you what I mean.

Monday – She flew out yesterday afternoon for a two-week training session in Illinois, but at least she's allowed to come home over the weekend. Until then, I have a couple of things to handle.

Thing 1 is a charming-but-precocious, preternaturally smart seven-year-old with a penchant for stalling and losing focus on the world around him as he brings it all to bear on some fascinating fact in an almanac – or on something shiny.

Thing 2 is a deceptively cute, street-smart three-year-old who reveals an evil glint in his eyes whenever he smiles at me, and who has an appetite for sugar and destruction.

My daily mission is to wake them, dress them, feed them, drop them off, go to work, pick them up, feed them, bathe them, dress them and get them to bed. It might not sound so bad, but with my wife out of town, you have to understand – the total parental manpower in this household has been reduced by a good 75-80 percent....

She pre-arranged as much as she possibly could, to make the tasks easier for me. Part of me wanted to be offended by the patronizing aspect of that, but most of me was grateful.

I have to say, though, that it reminded me of those weeks during high school when Mom and Dad had to leave town, and they sort of "trusted" me to take care of the place in their absence. Mom would stack the freezer with pre-cooked meals, in order by weekday, with a menu and cooking instructions taped to the front of the freezer door. Dad would leave a note along the lines of, "No parties, no drinking, no girls!"

My wife did most of that, but forgot to forbid parties and girls. Either she knows she can trust me, or she knows I'll be too exhausted to misbehave.

The difficulties were sure to start at breakfast. For whatever reason, our boys are hooked on instant grits. I don't know who introduced them to instant grits, but I hope that person doesn't expect my gratitude.

I hate instant grits – not their taste, but their very presence. They are impossible to clean up and if left unchecked, will multiply like Tribbles. Whenever Thing 2 finishes with breakfast, he has grits down his shirt, up his nose, on the table, on the floor, on his sleeves, on the cat, in his lap, in his shoes, in his hair and between his fingers. It often looks like there are more messes than there were grits to begin with.

And every attempt to clean them is fruitless. You just can't get rid of them. Use a wet paper towel and they absorb the water and grow. Use a dry one and you simply push them from one undesirable location to another. They are one of the few things in our house that will make me curse like my dad used to do.

But the boys love them, and grits manage to give them a warm, nutritional breakfast that's not packed with sugar. So my wife forbears and offers to handle making – and cleaning up – their grits each morning. Doing so this week, however, would entail a fairly pesky commute for her.

So it was going to fall to me. Knowing the extent of my desperation, she went to great lengths to help me avoid dealing with grits in her absence. It's called bribery.

She told the boys they'd get to do "special" breakfasts over the next two weeks, allowing them to pick out a variety of those round, allegedly single-serving containers of sugared cereal: Frosted Flakes, Lucky Charms, Apple Jacks and Frosted Mini-Wheats – their dentist's dream come true.

We figured I wouldn't have to deal with the grits, but I also wouldn't have to deal with the sugar highs. If they eat the cereal in the car, I can drop them off before the rush kicks in – then they become their teachers' problems.

Thing 2 loved this idea. He was especially excited about the Apple Jacks, holding one of the containers and singing "Ackle Jack, Ackle Jack!" as loudly as he could while he sat in the grocery cart the other night. He wanted to open them immediately, but my wife explained they're for breakfasts after she goes to Peoria.

She wasn't a minute out of our neighborhood when he asked, "Daddy, Mommy gone to Pee-oowa?" I answered him and was worried about his reaction for a second – I thought he was going to cry because he was already missing her. Instead, he shouted, "Yay! Now we hab Ackle Jack!"

"No, Sugarbear, those aren't for an afternoon snack; those are for breakfast."

"Den I want bepfuss now."

"No, breakfast is for morning.

"Den I want Ackle Jack for snack."

"Oh, look – it's the Wii! Have I shown you how to play this yet?"

I was proud of myself for the rest of the afternoon, distracting him with a videogame babysitter and addressing the issue whenever he remembered to bring it up. It takes a firm stance and insistence that Apple Jacks are not a good snack, that they are for a specific meal.

Unfortunately, that meal turned out to be dinner. The Things enjoyed it, though, and were more than cooperative for the rest of the night.

Once I put them to bed, I set about planning this morning's routine, only to discover that she'd left precious little to plan. She'd packed my car with a week's worth of daycare supplies, a spare pair of Diego underwear (not mine) and ten commute snacks. I grabbed a school snack to put in Thing 1's backpack, but it already had a week's worth in its pocket, plus a note instructing me to open the fridge, take out the perishable lunch items that she couldn't pack in advance and add them (at the rate of one each morning) to said backpack.

I shook my head and smiled to myself as I put the backpack down and returned the unneeded snack to the pantry. I was closing the pantry door when something caught my eye. There were still five days' worth of cereal cups on the shelf.

After caving on the Apple Jacks, I thought I was doomed. We'd used a day's worth of cereal, so I figured I'd be leading the charge in a grit battle for at least one morning.

But there, among the microwaveable dinners stacked in order by weekday, I spotted an extra pair of cereal cups. Apple Jacks, like Manna from Mommy. I halfway expected to see a Dad-like note along the lines of, "No caving!"

Tuesday – This morning, the call was for Lucky Charms, which of course means Thing 2 picked out and ate the marshmallow bits from the top of his cup before declaring he was "finish." But I knew he wouldn't go hungry, since his daycare provides a real breakfast; his weekday morning meal at home is more like a pre-breakfast snack.

Because Thing 1 doesn't get breakfast at school, I had to do a better job with him and make sure he ate enough to get through the morning. To that end, I told him to eat *all* of the marshmallow bits, not just the ones on top.

I also discovered why my wife insists on keeping the television off every weekday morning; watching it is counterproductive, as "Blue's Clues" is a distraction from eating. But I managed to wolf something down during a commercial break.

The drive to school started with the Things arguing over what song I should play on my iPod. Each has a current favorite, based on its intro. Seems they both love count-ins.

Thing 2 enjoys Paul McCartney's spirited "One-Two-Three-FAH!" from "I Saw Her Standing There" and requests it ad nauseum. He rarely waits for the song to end before requesting it again. In fact, he rarely waits for the first verse to begin before asking me to start the song over. So it's no surprise that he'd barely said, "Pay duh Beedles' Yun-too-fee-fore" before Thing 1 began to loudly voice his objection.

Thing 1 knows Spanish, and enjoys shouting out "Hola!" and "Donde esta?" during the chorus of U2's "Vertigo." He also thinks it's hilarious that Bono said "fourteen" instead of "four" during the count-in, so he regularly requests "that song that starts off 'unos, dos, tres, catorce.'" But as soon as he made the friendly suggestion that we play it instead of his brother's choice, the screaming match was on.

I tried for a compromise, but my suggestion of the Wiggles was met by further screaming. Frantically turning the click wheel to find anything that might appease both screamers, I failed to notice the brake lights ahead of me in a timely manner. I looked up in time to prevent an accident, but only at the cost of multiple skidmarks – both outside and inside the car – and an airborne iPod. I couldn't reach it under the dashboard, so we made the rest of the drive with no count-ins.

I did, however, get my wish – the arguing stopped immediately. Then, for the rest of the drive, there was even some sibling cooperation. Amazing how they can put aside their differences for the sake of a unified show of criticism of my poor driving skills....

Wednesday – Breakfast rations are dwindling, and I fear I'll have to break out the dreaded grits by week's end. My little cereal killer continues to ravage the pantry, despite my continued insistence that the individual servings are not a sustainable resource. To get more would entail shopping.

I can't shop while they're in school, because I have to work. And I can't shop at night, because I'd rather feed them lint than take them into a grocery store by myself. I'd be outnumbered, and my zone defense is not that good. Hence, the cereal must last.

This was supposed to be Frosted Mini-Wheats Day for each of them. Part of my wife's pre-departure counseling was: Never give either son a chance to claim that the other is receiving preferential treatment. Anything other than strict adherence to these guidelines may result in sheer chaos and a complete breakdown of familial infrastructure.

To that end, they are to be given the same thing during the same sitting – the same-sized portions of the same type of product (made by the same brand) with the same size, shape and color of auxiliary utensils. (As is a servant's tradition, I am to eat in separate quarters at another time.) Quite simply, one brother may not have milk in a blue cup if the other has juice in a red cup, or if Daddy has amber liquid in a clear bottle.

And so, I announced to both of them that they would be having Frosted Mini-Wheats, which was met with much rejoicing. Until Thing 2 tried some.

"Daddy, I don't yike dese."

"That's all we have, Sugarbear."

"I saw Yucky Charms in dere." He pointed an accusing finger at the pantry door.

Busted, and sensing an addiction-fueled tantrum of monumental proportions, I lapsed into bargaining mode. Some people consider bargaining to be a parent's biggest mistake, but it can be a necessity when time doesn't allow for kicking and screaming. And I didn't have time to engage in either of those activities.

There are people who will tell you it's a sign of weakness to let a crying child have his way. They will insist that a screaming, pitching, reeling toddler can be brought into instant submission with a quick swat. They will swear that every time a child wins, an angel loses its wings.

There's a word for the people who tell you these things: *childless.*

The unfortunate truth about parenting is that sometimes it requires a firm stance, sometimes it requires skilled negotiation and sometimes it requires a white flag. The critical element to this equation is knowing how/when to choose one's battles. With a scant 30 minutes until work was going to start, including 25 minutes of driving and drop-offs, I chose wisely.

When I make such a choice, all I have to think about is the human skeleton. Specifically, joints. Joints make it possible for the human body to bend. Bending makes it possible for the human body to sit. Sitting is the only legal way to transport a human toddler's body. But when Thing 2 has a tantrum, none of this is possible.

He has the freaky ability to simultaneously, irrevocably lock every joint in his body. Once they are locked, nothing and no one can bend them again until Thing 2 is good and ready for them to bend. His body goes completely rigid – stiff and straight as a two-by-four.

Have you ever tried to strap a two-by-four into a booster seat in the back of a car? I have, and it's a painful memory.

But it's a memory that came back to me while I was watching a tantrum about to unfold, at the same time that I was watching the clock. Snap decision – the kid wins this time and everybody's happy. There's no rule saying I can't punish him later – isn't that what bedtime ghost stories are for?

Decision made, addiction fed and chaos abated, I turned to his brother to make sure I hadn't just invited further trouble by offering them different menus.

"Doodlebug, I'm giving your brother tomorrow's Junkie Charms, but there's still a cup left for you. He'll have to eat something else tomorrow – possibly lint."

"*Junkie* Charms? Don't you mean Lucky Charms, Dad?"

"No, son. No, I don't."

"Then what does 'Junkie' mean?"

"Ask your mother."

"But she's not here! Did you forget she's in Peoria?"

"No, son. No, I didn't...."

Thursday – I'd rather not talk about breakfast today. For dinner, though, I learned a thing or two about our frozen entrees. We found some tasty frozen pasta meals that they love, but I'm all-thumbs in the kitchen. These things have their cooking instructions printed on the bottom – several steps' worth. The first step is to pull back the top cover and microwave the box for three minutes. That was easy enough.

But I can never remember Step 2. It's something to do with stirring certain ingredients separately; these things have pasta, cheese sauce and occasionally something akin to meat. They are to be kept separate from one another in Steps 2 and 3. It's easy to keep them separate when they're frozen solid, but that's prior to the completion of Step 1.

At the onset of Step 2, the cook is left with three partially runny lumps in the same box, with no dividers. Yet the lumps must be stirred and kept from mixing with the other lumps. This is something like putting three raw eggs in a bowl, then telling somebody to break the yoke of one and stir it up, without disturbing the other two eggs.

Further complicating matters is the fact that, as of Step 2, the cook has an open container of freshly microwaved partial liquids, with further instructions on the bottom. That's where I ran into trouble.

I was certain Step 2 had something to do with mixing, but I wasn't sure what. So I turned the container over, to read the bottom.

On my second attempt, after having wiped macaroni wheels off the stove, I remembered the container was open. This time, I held it up in the air in order to read the instructions from below.

Know what? Microwaved macaroni cheese burns when it drips in your eye.

For attempt number 3, I got smart and grabbed a pencil and an unpaid bill, the back of which made for an excellent blank note page. I grabbed another frozen meal out of the freezer, turned it over, and started writing steps 2-4 on the back of the envelope. I was still on step 3 when I realized I didn't need to make notes; all I had to do was read the back of a still-frozen one while working with a hot one.

Frozen crib notes in hand, I followed steps 2-4 on the next batch of macaroni wheels. Stir the runny masses, but don't let them mix! Reheat for another minute to 90 seconds. Stir everything together. Allow to cool sufficiently before serving.

That last step is subjective, I discovered, and I still have the blisters on my thumbs to prove it. I'm not sure how a piece of crimped cardboard can retain so much heat, but Kwai Chang Caine could have used our cheeseburger mac to burn those dragon and tiger tattoos into his arms. I wound up with two long, red streaks on my thumbs, not resembling anything that even remotely suggests I'm a Shaolin priest with cool Kung Fu abilities. But I did manage to teach the boys a few new words.

Apart from my blistered thumbs and wounded pride, dinner seemed to go well. The boys were well-behaved, the food was enjoyable once it cooled down, and Blue gave some good clues to Steve about her missing ball.

Then came bathtime. Something else I'm not ready to talk about yet, but I have to admit that Thing 2's logic was spot on — a quick shot of soapy water from a spitting rubber duck *is* a good way to flush the cheese sauce from Daddy's burnt eye....

Friday – Having come to the conclusion that Daddy-made meals are not the best arrangement, I decided to take the boys out for dinner.

"Who wants hamburgers?" I called out from the driver's seat as we left the school parking lot.

"MEEEE!" they shrilled in unison. Now we were talking. For the first time this week, we'd agreed on a meal. Then I made the mistake of offering options.

"Where should we go?"

"McDurgerKing!" came the discordant response. Their heads turned simultaneously for the inevitable staredown. I watched the rearview mirror in horror, anticipating the explosion.

"No! BurgDonald's!" Their eyes narrowed as I silently counted backward from five.

"DADDY! He won't let me go where I want!" was about all I could discern; then the screaming turned into something like, "Bleeeee-argle-karchem-chopfork!" as each struggled to make his voice heard above the other's.

As we approached a red light, I took a moment to breathe, then asked myself, What would Sweetie do? I could almost hear her voice inside my head, like Master Po: *Any parent can offer a compromise, Grasshopper. To win their submission, you must trick them into thinking they came up with it.*

"Cookies!" I said sharply. The buzzing sound from the backseat stopped.

"What, Daddy? What'd you say?"

"Nothing; you wouldn't be interested."

"No, tell me! Please? I thought you said 'cookies!'"

"I was just thinking, we're not too far from that cookie store at North Hills. Too bad there's not a burger place nearby, so we could stop there for dessert."

Then I waited for it.

"Hey! Daddy, there's a Five Guys there!"

"Fibe Guy!"

"Are y'all sure you'd want to eat at Five Guys?"

"Yes! Fibe Guys! Five Guy! Fibe Guys!"

I mentally thanked my wife as I turned in the direction of North Hills. We arrived in three happy moods, and I stood in line to order while the Things set out in search of a table to save. I forgot what this meant until the screaming started again. I looked up and saw them locked in a tug-of-war, each pulling the other's shirt with one hand while white-knuckling the edge of his preferred table with the other. The two tables were right next to each other and there was no discernible difference between them, except that each was chosen by the other brother. As they tugged on each other, they implored me, "This table! Dis table!"

Meanwhile, a non-supportive, non-sympathetic fellow dad was sitting at a table behind them, looking at me with a smirk on his face as if to say, *Are you going to handle this, or are you going to go ahead and put on a skirt?*

This was The Moment, then. All week, I'd been caving to their whims; I should have known that strategy would culminate in a public test of my mettle, a moment in which I'd have to prove my dadliness and actually take charge of a situation. I straightened my shirt, stepped out of line and marched over, prepared to do what it took to wipe that smirk off his face.

"BOYS!" I screamed in my loudest, angriest voice. They let go of each other in shock, each almost falling onto the table of his choice. "YOU'RE BOTHERING PEOPLE! STOP RIGHT NOW, OR NO BURGERS!" They went instantly silent, leaving only my angry voice as the distraction to other diners.

I knelt to their level, just like Supernanny says to do, and brought my voice to a calmer (but still stern) level: "Now listen. You just lost your right to pick a table; we're going to sit where *I* say. But first, you're going to come back and stand in line with me, where you'll be quiet, be patient and behave."

I stood up before the chorus of "Aww, man!" could start, whirled on one heel, and marched back to the line at the counter, where two people had already stolen my place. I turned and looked for the smirking dad, but he was nowhere to be seen. I had a moment of panic when I didn't see my sons, either, until I realized they were right behind me in single file – quiet, patient and behaving.

We ordered, paid and proceeded to the seats I chose, where I looked around again for the Smirker. No luck. He'd been in the middle of a half-pound of cheeseburger when I'd first noticed him; there was no way he could have finished and left during the 30-second conflict and resolution that had taken my attention from him. I could only conclude that he'd been either a messenger sent to provoke The Moment or an hallucination brought on by sheer exhaustion. I didn't care which, as the three of us sat and enjoyed our dinner together.

Thing 2 even waited until he truly was finished before claiming to be finished. At that point, he got out of his chair in order to perform The Dance. This is something of a restaurant tradition for him – if the PA is playing anything lively, he'll seek out a wide patch of table-free space in which to dance. It's unlike any motion I've ever seen, and I'm not sure words can do it justice. He'll sort of pitch and reel, turning on his heels while he shakes his hips and wiggles his arms like a mini-Elvis who's about a half-beat off from the actual rhythm of the song. It's strange, but also strangely entertaining.

The Dance never fails to elicit smiles from nearby adults, which is probably his motivation for performing again the next time we eat out. The middle-aged woman across the aisle from us watched for a moment in startled bemusement before her face broke into a large grin. I don't know if she was smiling at the moves themselves, or the fact that a three-year-old was dancing to George Thorogood's "Bad To The Bone."

Even the added attention wasn't enough to foul the mood of Thing 1, who normally tires of The Dance within 10 seconds and insists that Thing 2 return to his seat at once and stop embarrassing everybody. This time, all he did was make eye contact with the woman across the aisle, shake his head, shrug and say, "Little brothers!"

With bellies full and behavior reigned in, we left Five Guys for the cookie store, then sat on a bench near the Commons to enjoy the summer evening. Thing 1 told me corny jokes while Thing 2 shouted compliments on the driving skills of various passers-by: "Good turning, Man! Nice stopping, Girl!"

Thing 1 was between punchlines when he realized he and Thing 2 were the only ones eating cookies. "Daddy! Don't you want dessert?"

"No thanks, Doodlebug. I'm too busy savoring the sweet taste of being in control."

"You're weird, Dad."

"Sure I am, son, sure I am. Did I mention your mother's coming back tonight?"

Saturday – Woke up at 3am to the sound of crying from across the hall, for the third night in a row. The first night, it was due to thunder. The second, a coughing fit. I didn't know what had scared him this time but as I sat up to get out of bed and go comfort him, I beheld a flaxen-haired vision arising from the other side of the mattress. She'd apparently returned some time after I'd passed out on top of the bedspread, and hadn't awakened me.

"I got this one," she whispered, and I listened for Thing 2's surprised reaction when he realized who was coming into his room.

The crying stopped almost immediately, and I heard him say, "Mommy! You came home?"

They talked in low voices for a few minutes, but I knew there was no way he was going back to sleep in his own bed. In fact, there was probably no way he'd do anything without her for the next 48 hours.

She carried him in and set him next to me on the bed, whereupon he started bouncing on his knees, digging his elbows into my ribs and informing me repeatedly that Mommy was home.

"Let Daddy go back to sleep, Sugarbear," she admonished gently as she slipped under the covers next to him. He obeyed immediately, turned to her for a nose-deep-in-the-clavicle snuggle, and settled in for the long haul.

"Thanks for taking such good care of them this week," she whispered.

"No problem," I mumbled. "They've been good."

"So you really don't mind doing it all over again next week?"

"..."

"Dan?"

"..."

"I guess Daddy's already asleep again, Sugarbear...."

- August 2008

82

A Nay for Effort

Period 6:
Computer Science

Computers are getting smarter all the time: scientists
tell us that soon they will be able to talk to us.
(By they I mean computers: I doubt scientists will
ever be able to talk to us.)

– Dave Barry

Labored Day

The other day I called my computer helpline, because I needed to be made to feel ignorant by someone much younger than me.

– Bill Bryson

It should have been a fun holiday weekend – my wife's temporary return to Raleigh, my temporary return to sanity and three days off to temporarily catch up on everything I hadn't been able to do while she'd been out of town. Like answering the 300+ email messages that had built up over the past week, writing for some recent assignments or backing up my hard drive (cue ominous foreshadow music).

But the polo people had other plans for me....

I'm talking about the employees at those big electronics stores – the ones with clever, alliterative names like Superlative Sale or Technical Town – who wear matching polo shirts and earn matching salaries, without even a hint of commission or incentive. They wander the aisles, oblivious to customers or anything related to us...including service.

Some of them even purport to work in a service department, which is generally set up to resemble a cage or a pen. This is no coincidence.

I spent the better part of the weekend pacing one such cage, hoping the keepers would throw me a bone. By Monday evening, I felt as if I'd performed the Twelve Labors of Hercules...or six of them, anyway.

The weekend started well enough; everybody slept in. We had a leisurely Saturday morning, even when the monitor fizzled out on my laptop. This concerned me, but I figured it just meant I'd have to buy a new video card. So we added a stop at Superlative Sale to our agenda, following haircuts for the boys and dinner at our favorite pizza place.

The haircut appointment was a huge success; we've discovered a place that specializes in cuts for children, offering an indoor playground, videogames and lollipops. These things inspire a kid to behave while he's sitting in a barber's seat (especially if it's shaped like an airplane or a motorcycle, which theirs are).

Feeling brave after their good behavior, we took them into the drugstore next door, where we had to buy a lottery scratcher and a new bottle of Sesame Street bubble bath. While I was waiting to pay, Doodlebug grew bored and began jumping backwards up the aisle. After a quick admonishment, he got that typical look of incredulity on his face, and said, "What? This is my trick!"

Whereupon his younger brother, who has difficulty with consonant blends, decided to mimic him in as loud of a voice as possible: "Yeah, Daddy! And dis is *my* dick!"

The clerk dropped the bubble bath onto the floor, even as I wanted to disappear into it. "Trick! It's your trrrrick!" I enunciated loudly. "Okay, boys, you oughta get going; why don't you and Mommy wait for me outside?"

"But Daddy! I wanna show 'em my dick!"

Their mother quickly scooped one under each arm and headed for the door. By the time we made it to dinner, we were able to laugh about it. Not so with the tricks pulled by the polo people at Superlative Sale later....

When my laptop monitor first went out, it started with a multi-colored flare of fuzzy vertical lines – resembling a laughing mouth, now that I think about it – then went dark. I hit every key I could think of, turned it off with the power switch, plugged it into an outlet, plugged an external monitor into it and tried again. Multiple times.

I left it alone for 30 minutes, then tried again, just in case it was an issue of overheating. In short, I tried everything I could think of. Which is why I was surprised when Superlative Sales' tech support guy suggesting popping out the battery as a solution.

The First Labor:

I'd been waiting for about 25 minutes, the first of half a dozen such waits inside the customer corral that I'll think of forevermore as the home of the Weak Squad. Finally, a polo-clad kid resembling John Lennon circa The White Album nodded to me, as if I should be glad of the opportunity to consult with him. I think he might have expected me to approach the counter with respect and trepidation; I did neither. I simply placed the laptop in front of him and told him the monitor had gone out, although the CPU still seemed to be working.

His first move was to turn on the laptop, ostensibly to verify that the monitor truly was inoperable. As if I'd have been there otherwise. If I ever wait in line for that long just to have someone point out that everything is fine and I simply hadn't turned on the laptop, I hope my wife will seriously consider breaking out my living will and insisting on her right to pull my plug.

Needless to say, the laptop turned on and the monitor stayed dark. His next tactic was to pop out the battery and walk away. He must have seen the quizzical look on my face, because he deigned to toss an explanation over his shoulder: "Sometimes it helps to remove the battery for five minutes, then put it back in."

This is the equivalent of the standard corporate IT solution: "Try rebooting it."

I think the guy just wanted a bathroom break. Whatever the case, he came back in fifteen minutes, put the battery in, and turned on the laptop again. Still no monitor.

"Want us to run a diagnostic?" he queried in his most helpful tone.

"The thought had occurred to me," I said in my most dumbfounded.

"Okay, well, we're a little backed up right now, so just to let you know, it could take 7-14 days before we get to it."

My mind reeled at the thought of losing My Precious for two weeks. He continued as if he had not just delivered a verbal kick to my solar plexus.

"Our standard diagnostic is $69, but if you want us to back up your hard drive first to prevent loss of data, that's an extra $99."

"Why would there be a risk of losing data if you're just diagnosing it?"

"You never know, sir – we take these things apart, and anything could happen," he said with a shrug, reminding me of a movie hood collecting protection money. Knowing what happens when someone refuses to pay their protection money, I agreed.

"If money's an issue, some of it might be covered in your warranty. I'd need to see a receipt to know for sure; we can print one here in the store."

"Sure, that sounds good; why don't you print one up and let me know?"

"They can do that for you in Customer Service, sir."

"Isn't that where I am?"

"No, this is Technical Service. Customer Service is over there," he said, indicating another winding line of beleaguered-looking customers.

So I trudged the 20 feet to the other side of the pen, waited my turn, argued with the Customer Service clerk about the exact meaning of "I bought it in late December or early January," and finally got my receipt. Clutching it like a trophy, I walked back to Technical Service, where John Lennon was now elbow-deep in some poor soul's CPU. I sat and waited another 15 minutes for him to tell them there was nothing he could do to help, then showed him the proof of warranty.

He waived the $69 diagnostic fee, but kept the $99 charge for what would essentially amount to popping my hard drive into another computer, typing "Copy C:/*.*" and walking away for an hour. But without a monitor to show me what I was typing and whether my external drive was hooked up, I couldn't do the same thing; therefore, he had the law of supply and demand on his side.

Before proceeding with the backup, he gave me a sheet of paper and asked me to list the files that were most important to me. I wrote, "All of them."

I asked him how long it would take to perform the backup, and if there was any way I could have access to those files earlier in the 7-14 day range necessary for the diagnostic step. They could keep the laptop for as long as they wanted, but I needed to retrieve my latest files so I could possibly continue working on them on a different computer. He assured me it was all part of the same 7-14 days, and that there was no way of knowing how soon my data would be backed up. I winced at the cold reference to my articles as "data," then turned and began to walk away.

I stopped to watch an argument unfolding between another customer and service tech. The customer was unhappy because he'd bought a new computer, purchased their data transfer service and dropped off his old computer for said transfer, only to have it go missing.

What stood out in my mind, though, was that the customer had just bought the new PC the previous night – seemed they were willing to transfer data in less than 7-14 days, after all. I ran to the car and asked my wife if she still wanted to get a low-end PC for the boys for Christmas, and if so, whether she'd like to buy it early...and give me a chance to try it out.

The Second Labor:

Twenty minutes later, I got to the front of the tech support line, where I asked a more helpful support guy if it was true they would transfer the contents of an old PC to a new one that had been purchased at their store. I told him my laptop was already checked in and said I'd be right back with a new PC.

Thirty minutes later, I again reached the front of the line, cheap new CPU in hand. I managed to time this visit so I wound up talking to the same helpful guy, who now needed extensive reminders of who I was.

He had no memory of having spoken to me half an hour before, but again verified that they could transfer the contents of my laptop to the new computer. When he asked if 3pm the next day would be acceptable, I decided to dedicate my first novel to him.

The Third Labor:

At 3:35pm Sunday, I reached the front of the tech support line, where a third support rep typed my name into the system and confirmed that the new CPU was ready, complete with my old data. I had a moment's panic when he began searching the pile of boxes for pickup and said he couldn't find it, but he managed to literally stumble across it just around the corner from the pile.

I had to suppress a laugh when I saw that one of the boxes in the pile had the words "Who's is this?" written across it. At least I wasn't the poor sap who was hoping to pick that one up today....

Rep #3 finished closing out my ticket, bent over to pick up the box with my new computer inside and instantly looked confused. I leaned over the counter and discovered what was confusing him – the box still had its original packing tape on it. My face fell as I heard myself saying, "They haven't loaded it yet."

He explained that Rep #2 obviously had left it in the wrong place – around the corner from the customer pickups, where nobody had noticed it. I pointed out that he'd practically tripped over it, adding that I couldn't understand how it had seemed so invisible the previous night.

I interrupted his apologies to explain that my wife would be leaving the next day at noon, and that it would be difficult for me to pick up the PC after that. He said he would personally ensure that the transfer took place before morning, even if he had to stay and do it himself. As I plodded away, I realized I was beginning to feel more like Sisyphus than Hercules.

The Fourth Labor:

Monday morning, I drove over at opening time, stood in line for the requisite 20 minutes, and introduced myself to the fourth new face behind the counter. He looked up my paperwork and apologized that they hadn't had time to transfer the files the night before, adding that it would only take 30-60 minutes, "if we can just locate the backup drive." He advised me to "go get some lunch" and come back, whereupon the new PC would be as full as I was.

I called my wife, knowing she had to go to the airport in 90 minutes, to ask if she needed me for anything prior to her departure. She reassured me she was packed and ready, and gave me her blessing to go have some breakfast in the same shopping center and wait for the PC to be ready.

With 30 minutes to go, I approached the counter apprehensively. Rep #2, whose memory hadn't improved in 36 hours, was surprised to learn that his teammates had been unable to handle a simple data transfer. He wondered aloud who could have left the box in the wrong place, shrugged it off and went to check on transfer progress. He returned with apologies and an explanation that the files were still copying, but that it would only be a few more minutes.

"I can't afford to wait that long; I have to take my wife to the airport," I explained through gritted teeth.

He apologized again and promised to look into getting me a refund for my troubles.

"Thank you, but I have to warn you – I'd hoped it wouldn't come to this, but you brought it on yourselves – when I come back, I'll have two rambunctious little boys with me. They're going to want to show everyone their tricks and will probably inflict all manners of chaos while I wait in line."

"We'll have it boxed up and ready to go, sir!" he clamored with a mixture of ambition and fear.

"Don't bother!" I called back over my shoulder. "I'll want to see it in order to verify that you really did transfer the data!"

The Fifth Labor:

After many anguished good-byes and buckets of tears at the airport, I managed to pull the boys away from the playground and observation deck, heading off for a quick lunch and what I hoped would be my last trip to Superlative Sale this weekend. I loaded the three-year-old into his stroller/restraint device, threatened the seven-year-old with multiple foul consequences if he even thought to utter the words "I'm bored," gave each of them an old handheld electronic game and took them inside to wait in the cage.

I was pleasantly surprised to see our new PC set up on the tech support counter, hooked up to a monitor. After I waited 20 minutes in line, a supervisor took me to the monitor, proud to show me what they'd transferred for me. I asked him about my refund, and he said he was surprised to hear anyone had offered me one, since he was the only one on duty who could authorize refunds and it wasn't his policy to offer them to make up for long waits. I overlooked this in the sheer glee at seeing actual files listed on the monitor.

"Did you manage to get my e-mail file?" I asked.

"As long as it was in its default location, which would be 'My Documents.' Take a look at this, sir, and let me know if we missed anything else you wanted transferred."

"Well, yes – you missed My Documents."

"Your documents are right there, sir, under 'Miscellaneous.'"

"No, I don't mean 'my documents.' I mean 'My Documents' – the standard Windows folder called 'My Documents.' It's not there. 'Miscellaneous' is one of the sub-folders, but we had several others. I wanted to see everything from 'My Documents.'"

"We can't transfer everything from 'My Documents' because there could be corrupt data, and that would mess up your new PC."

"There was no corrupt data! I didn't come in here with a data problem; I came in with a monitor problem! I expected everything to be transferred from 'My Documents' Saturday night, and you still haven't transferred it, two days later!"

The boys looked up from their handhelds to watch me in wonder; even they had never heard this tone of anger from me before.

"Well, these things take time, sir, and we're very backed up right now."

"Don't tell me now that they take time! Your team told me Saturday that they could do it by 3pm Sunday! They promised me this, knowing how backed up they were at the time – their failure has nothing to do with how long the job took; it has to do with how long they put it off! I want my files on this machine right now!"

"Sir, I understand your anger, but it's going to take some time. I'll go pull the backup drive –"

"Assuming you can find it."

"– and look into this myself. I've seen you now; I'll remember you when you come back –"

"Like Rep Number 2 did?"

"– and I'll personally have your data ready, but you have to give me time."

"Time is one thing I don't have; I have kids. Come on, boys, we're leaving!"

I whirled on one foot, nearly upset the stroller as I grabbed it and tried to turn it toward the exit, and marched away fully knowing I'd probably regret my outburst later, but feeling oddly balanced in the mean time.

The Sixth Labor:
By 6pm, I still hadn't heard from The Supervisor, so I called him to ask if my PC was ready. He seemed surprised that I'd waited so long to contact him, since it had been ready two hours ago. I nearly threw the phone across the room, thought better of it and once again dragged the boys off to Superlative Sale.

The cage was eerily quiet as we approached, and I was shocked to see there was no line. The Supervisor was waiting for me, and began his spiel before I even reached the counter. He'd found an additional 50GB of data, which he'd personally scrubbed before transferring. Normally, that would cost more than the usual $99 backup fee but he was willing to forego those charges in light of extenuating circumstances. I bit my tongue as I checked the data, approved it, signed, grabbed the PC and left.

He offered me a handcart for the PC, but I explained that I couldn't push that and the stroller. The hint was lost on him, so I asked Doodlebug to push his brother in the stroller as I carried the box toward the exit. Security stopped me to check my receipt, just to make sure I wasn't shoplifting. I had to suppress my first response, but I'm glad I did; that security guard wound up being the friendliest, most helpful employee I'd met there all weekend.

I wished him a Happy Labor Day as we walked away.

- September 2008

Serenity Theft

Ask not for whom the bell tolls; let the answering machine get it.
– Jean Kerr

S ome "management" company has been calling us daily for the past several weeks. Every night, our caller ID shows at least one call came in from them during the day, but they never leave a message. Finally last weekend, we were here when they called. Suspecting a telemarketer, I had our two-year-old at the ready, because I really enjoy giving those calls to him.

It was a recording. If there's one thing worse than being called by a telemarketer, it's being called by an answering machine. "Please press '1' for an important business message, or call us at the following number." Not only is this group bothering me on my weekend, they want me to do all the work, too. I took the bait anyway.

I pressed '1' and the call connected remarkably quickly, considering it went to India. Someone answered, and I'm pretty sure he asked how he could help me. I said, "I don't know – you called me."

He asked for my name – again, surprising. I figured an outsourced management service would have better technology than I have in my home, yet I knew who'd called me and he didn't.

When I gave him my name, he looked up the account and told me it's a matter for my wife. I passed the phone to her, wondering how many keys she would have to press to find out what these people wanted.

It turns out, they wanted to talk to her about a past-due bill from Cingular. The account is in collections. She told him she doesn't have a Cingular account, and the phone call was disconnected. "I think he hung up on me," she said.

"Could be the broken cables that interrupted service over there last week."

"That only affected Internet service."

"How do you know you weren't on the Internet? You might have been talking to a website rather than a person. Those outsourcers are pretty thrifty that way."

But we chalked the whole thing up to the other Bains. There's a woman in another North Carolina town who has my wife's name and apparently doesn't pay her bills on time. As far as we can tell, she's not guilty of identity theft – she never claimed to be my wife and never used my wife's social security number. She simply has the same first and last name. You'd think it takes more than that to link a person to an account. You'd be wrong.

Consider something that happened a few months ago, when an angry gentleman called and asked to speak to my wife. Not only am I nice to my wife, I also get a perverse sense of joy in messing with jerks. So I ran interference.

I told him she wasn't home and asked what this was about. "Personal matter," he mumbled.

"What kind of personal matter?"

"She home or not?"

"Depends. Who's calling?"

"Personal financial matter."

"I can handle it; I'm her husband."

"This bill's in her name."

"The bank account's in mine."

"You authorized to handle her finances?"

"You think I'm gonna say 'No' at this point?"

"She owes money on her Best Buy account."

"She doesn't have a Best Buy account. I do, though."

"Then you owe money on your Best Buy account."

"Then why did you ask to talk to my wife?"

"Because it's in her name."

"Then it's not my account. Again, my wife doesn't have a Best Buy account. I do, and her name isn't on it. Plus, I paid it two weeks ago. You must have us confused with the other Bains."

"Sir, lemme talk to your wife."

"She doesn't want to talk to you."

"Then she *is* home?"

"It doesn't matter. She doesn't have a Best Buy account. But I bet the other Bains do. Maybe you should call and harass them."

"You sayin' this isn't your account?"

"Neither mine nor my wife's."

"Right. Prove it, then. What's your account number?"

"I'm not giving you my account number! What's the number of the past-due account? I'll tell you if it's not mine."

"I can't give you that number; it might not belong to your wife."

"Then you admit you've called the wrong person?"

"Lemme talk to your wife."

"She's busy. Would you like to talk to our son?"

Click.

One quick call to the Best Buy folks, and the matter was resolved. They called off their dog and sicced him on the other Bains. My account was not past due, but the collection agency never bothered to verify account numbers. Or social security numbers. Or even phone numbers. Instead, they found the first person to pop up with my wife's name – namely, my wife.

So why are we outsourcing collection jobs when we can do them just as badly over here? Any American can pick up a phone book and call the first match on a name – it doesn't take an outlander with an American PhD to do that. Then again, if someone's going to get testy and threaten to come after us for payments due, I'm glad to know they're half a world away and the threat is hollow.

Meanwhile, our Cingular saga continued Monday evening, when we came home to the old familiar caller ID tag. Their management company was still trying to reach us! I wasn't sure what they were managing at that point, other than to annoy us.

But I offered to call them for her, thinking maybe I could manage something, too. I tried the next morning after she'd left for work.

"Thank you for calling _____ Management. This call may be monitored and recorded for quality assurance." (In retrospect, I really, really hope they were monitoring that one.)

"Hi, you've been calling us about an account we don't have."

"Okay, sir, I can look that up. What number are we calling you from?"

"What number are *you* calling *me* from?"

"Yes, sir."

"Calling me *from* or calling me *at*?"

"Calling you from."

"Are you sure? You want to know what number *you're* calling from, or did I misunderstand you?"

"What number are we calling you from, sir?"

"That would be your number – whatever number you're at. I guess it's the one I just dialed."

"No, sir, I need to know what number we've been calling you from."

"I just told you."

"No, you told me *our* number."

"Right. *Your* number is the number *you've* been calling *from*. That's what you asked me for. I assume you actually want to know *my* number?"

"Yessss." Her tone of voice cannot possibly be duplicated via the written word, but try to imagine talking to someone who thinks you're the stupidest person alive.

"Just trying to clarify matters. You did ask for your number. But my number is..." and I rattled off our digits, wondering how in the world she felt she had a right to be disgusted with me when she was the one lacking communication skills.

"Okay, I'll look that up. What did we say in our message?"

"You didn't leave a message. You've called every day for weeks, but you never leave a message. One guy got through and said it's about a cellular bill, but we don't have a cellular phone. He got cut off, and the company's continued to—"

"I have it right here, sir. It's for a cellular bill in Mrs. Bain's name. Are you Mrs. Bain?"

"Are you kidding?"

"No."

"Neither am I. This is *Mr.* Bain."

"Is Mrs. Bain in?"

"No."

"Is there a number where we can reach her?"

"No. She doesn't have a cellular phone, remember?"

"Then can I leave my name and number?"

"No, she asked me to handle this. Besides, she already told the last guy that's not her account."

"It says here she owes $264, sir."

"She doesn't. It's not her account. You have the wrong Mrs. Bain."

"This is the phone number we have on record, sir, and the account associated with Mrs. Bain at this number is past due in the amount of $264. When can we expect payment, sir?"

"You can't. Unless you find the other Mrs. Bain, who's not at this number."

"Hold on, sir.... I'm showing the last four digits of Mrs. Bain's social security number as ____. Is that right?"

"Not for my Mrs. Bain. I already told you, you have the wrong person."

"But this is the phone number we have for the account."

"Then you have the wrong phone number. I've told you several times you've been calling the wrong Mrs. Bain."

"Sor-RY!" She stressed the second syllable to show her righteous indignation that we could dare to be the wrong Bains.

"That's okay, if you could just—"

Click.

She hung up on me! But at least I got the message across, I thought as I headed for work. I kept on thinking that, too – until we came home that night and found a very familiar listing on our caller ID....

That's fine. She doesn't have an account and they don't have her social, so they can call 'til they're blue in the automated message. They won't get any money from us, and they'll stop once Cingular realizes they've spent more than $264 to not recover $264.

So this time, it's harmless to us. But to the other Bains, I'd just like to say: if you ever have to borrow money from a loan shark to pay your other bills, please make sure he knows your address instead of ours.

- February 2008

Baitin' Switch

Analytical software enables you to shift human resources from rote data collection to value-added customer service and support where the human touch makes a profound difference.

– Bill Gates

Because a growing family equates to shrinking living space, we purged the contents of our home when we had our second son. This involved several tough decisions, a bit of furniture-moving and a lot of swearing.

Blindsided by a wifely strategy that still has me confused, I found myself purchasing *more* furniture to take up *less* space. But it worked, so I no longer argue.

Our new computer armoire closes up, looking nicer and requiring less space than the desks where our computers used to live. Unfortunately, it has less capacity for all of the extra equipment, junk and unpaid bills that were living there with them. Such squatters must be dealt with harshly.

We threw out some of the equipment, most of the junk and a couple of choice bills. This left two computers – the family desktop and the dedicated "writing" laptop that I stare at for several hours each night, hoping my muse will intervene with double shots of inspiration and espresso.

Deteriorating eyesight and oncoming carpal tunnel deterred me from using the laptop's tiny keyboard, monitor and mouse, so I used a set of larger peripherals much like the desktop had. But the new armoire doesn't have space for two sets of peripherals, so we were going to have to share one set – plus a printer – between both computers. My wife's only stipulation was she doesn't want to have to manually transfer a snake's nest of cords whenever she interrupts my laptop-staring to use the desktop.

Not to worry, I assured her. I think they make these little switch thingies for computers to share devices. If I can't find one, I'll just evacuate the armoire, store the laptop in my nightstand and suffer.

Thus began my nightmarish quest. It took two hours to discover the thingies' actual name on Google; they're called Keyboard-Video-Mouse-Peripheral (KVMP) switches and as it turns out, they're largely fictitious. Although I found a technology superstore whose website claimed they carry such a thing.

Armed with what I thought to be relevant information, I confidently entered their store the next day and immediately became lost in the chasms of computer equipment. A clerk less than half my age found me wandering and tried to help.

"Can I help you, sir?"

"I'm looking for a KVMP switch."

"You mean a KVM, sir?"

"No, I mean a KVMP."

"There's no such thing, sir."

"Sure there is; I found it on your website last night."

"Maybe you should order it from the site, then, sir."

Now I was getting miffed.

"I don't want to order it; I want to take one home today."

"You could take home one of our KVMs, sir."

"I've also got a P."

"The bathrooms are—"

"Don't," I growled. "The 'P' stands for peripheral – in my case it's a printer, something I imagine most computer users need?"

"Oh! You want a print server."

"Will that allow me to share a keyboard, monitor and mouse?"

"No, you'd need a KVM for that."

"Or a KVMP to accomplish both, with minimal equipment and capital outlay," I muttered through clenched teeth.

"What are you trying to set up, sir? Perhaps I can suggest an alternative."

"You don't need to know what I'm trying to set up; I know what I need and I'm looking for it, not suggestions."

A passing manager, fully half my age, heard my anguished tone and stopped to mollify me.

"Can I help you, sir?"

The clerk answered for me, "He's looking for a KVMP."

"There's no such thing, is there? You sure he didn't say KVM? Sir, what are you trying to set up?"

"He wants to share KVM, plus a printer."

"Oh! Did you show him our print servers?"

I walked out undetected as they continued to regurgitate their best customer service at one another.

After two trips to two similar superstores and two similar conversations with two similar polo-bedecked children, I admitted defeat, returned home and lived up to my promise. My laptop fits well in my nightstand, with enough space for some new glasses and carpal tunnel wristbands.

Although the kid at the drug store tried to convince me I need liniment instead.

- November 2007

Big Brother Is Sniffing You

My first psychiatrist said I was paranoid, but I want a second opinion because I think he's out to get me.

– Tom Wilson

This could be last column I write as a free man. I don't know if there will be word processors at Gitmo. (Or Nimby, or wherever the detainees are kept nowadays.) But I could soon find out.

After they drag me off for interrogations that may or may not be torturous, rest assured that, much like my column does for you, I'll never give them any practical information. I don't *have* any practical information, because I'm innocent of the thing they surely suspect me of.

It started with the airport searches. Last fall, when I was still gainfully employed instead of writing for a living, my boss sent me on a business trip to manage a video project. I flew with a videographer to multiple cities, prompting clients from off-camera to say nice things about our product. Unfortunately, we couldn't find enough clients willing to do that. But the first interviews had already been scheduled, so we had to book the others as we travelled – we literally didn't know where we would fly from one day to the next.

As it turns out, the airlines get suspicious of middle-aged men traveling in pairs with no return flight – who knew? Apparently, the automated sniffer did, because the ticketing computer flagged us for "random" searches.

We found ourselves spread-eagled in a holding pen while someone swabbed our shoes and checked us for ticklish spots. Still, in the name of national security, I was glad to see them being diligent...the first time. But the next day, at the next airport, they crossed the line from "diligent" to "unreasonable." It was the same airline, which I won't name here, as I wouldn't want to be dealt a lawsuit. But you'd think within the same company, the right hand would know what the left hand is doing. You'd be wrong.

Flagged again, I tried reminding Mr. Rubber Gloves that his colleagues across the country had already cleared me, and my safe arrival should have proven I wasn't a suicide bomber. He failed to see the logic; apparently, "zero tolerance" equates to "zero discretionary thought processes." But he cleared me in spite of his lack of logic, civility and ability to stand upright.

I haven't flown (or worked) since I finished that project, but I'm sure they're watching the passenger lists for my name, especially after the next incident. This one involved my second-grader, who's fascinated by geography, foreign languages and world events. He had a chance to research all three after another seven-year-old gave him the lowdown on the Middle East. He knew our troops are fighting *in* Iraq, which to him meant they're fighting *against* Iraq. He knows Iraq has a president; therefore as far as he's concerned, this man must be our enemy.

He also recently learned about Samantha Smith, the alliteratively named ten-year-old who appealed to Andropov to end the Cold War during the 80s (not to be confused with Ronald Reagan, the alliteratively named 76-year-old who appealed to Gorbachev to do the same). Emulating the former, my son took it upon himself one Saturday morning to write to Iraqi President Talabani in an appeal for peace.

I'd been letting him play Civilization, where he fancied he'd learned a thing or two about diplomacy (just call me Dad of the Year). Messengers in that videogame greet foreign dignitaries as "Most noble leader" and my little ambassador decided this would be a good start for his letter. But he didn't know if Talabani could read English, and wanted to translate it for him. Into Arabic. Online. Unsupervised. By using the search function I'd taught him to use (see my previous comment about Dad of the Year).

A few minutes later, he shouted upstairs that he couldn't find the Arabic word for "peace." Still half-asleep, I missed the obvious comeback and rolled over to ask him why he needed to know it. When he told me he was writing a letter to Iraq, I woke up the rest of the way. When he said he'd found an

Arabic dictionary online, I tripped on the sheets in my hurry to get to the computer.

Two bounds and a tumble later, I was downstairs, looking over my son's shoulder at an online forum called "Alburaq: Your Gateway to Palestine." I snatched the mouse from his hand, slammed the window closed, yanked the plug from the outlet and considered rubbing a magnet on the hard drive.

First things first, I explained to him that our war isn't with the new Iraqi president. When he asked who our enemy is, I told him to go ask his mother.

Next, I sat down to carefully consider my situation. I'm not even remotely Palestinian – heck, I think Hamas is just a chickpea spread served with pita chunks – but my IP address is now on record as having accessed a Palestinian chat room to translate the phrase "Most noble leader."

I may be paranoid, but I still know when I'm being watched. And there are Internet sniffers whose job it is to root out subversive online activities. It happened to another writer I know. For the sake of anonymity and obscure references, let's call him "Winston." One day, Winston posted a harmless joke on a private forum, responding to another colleague (whom we'll call "Syme"). But his joke contained a word that apparently attracts sniffers, even in an allegedly "private" forum. And once again, no one in authority felt independent enough to apply discretionary thought in the wake of zero tolerance.

The exchange started when Syme noticed a typo in one of Winston's messages and teased him about it, asking Winston what drugs he's on. Winston replied, "No drugs for me … I'm just high on life! And a little crystal meth. But mostly life!"

Everyone in the forum knew it was a joke. Without knowing Winston, outsiders surely know it was a joke. Maybe I'm just naïve about the drug scene, but I'm fairly certain that if one truly uses crystal meth, one doesn't broadcast that information online. But a sniffer picked up on the phrase, and someone somewhere took it seriously – the next day, two uniformed officers showed up on Winston's front porch. I kid you not.

They asked to come in "to talk," then once they were inside, broke the news that they'd like to look around for evidence of crystal meth. They found none, but they did find Winston's elderly parents, who live with him. The search thoroughly confused Winston's father, an Alzheimer's patient. At this point, the officers were forced to admit that maybe they had no business in this man's home. They left and never came back, but the RPD refused to tell Winston how they had been privy to his private post to begin with.

So Winston is safe for now, but I'm not sure the feds will be as forgiving of my son's online activity. I'm positive they're watching me right now; in fact, I'm writing this article to prove it. If I finish it without them kicking the door down, I might accept that I'm safe. But if I don't finish it, it probably means I've b

- July/August 2009

A Nay for Effort

Period 7:
Math/Statistics

I never did very well in math; I could never seem to
persuade the teacher that I hadn't meant
my answers literally.
— Calvin Trillin

A Lotta Rules for a Lottery

I figure you have the same chance of winning the lottery whether you play or not.

- Fran Lebowitz

Twenty months ago, I lost my job. I received a decent severance package and found a new job before it ran out (no, Jim, I'm not refunding the overlap) but it was a bitter pill to swallow, nonetheless. A layoff can be a serious blow to the male ego — I'm no biologist, but I'm pretty sure the hunter-gatherer instinct is embedded in the "Y" chromosome. There it sits, wrapped like a tiny burrito inside the pride gene, with testosterone generously sprinkled on top. You can't fight genetics, no matter how many sensitivity courses you've been forced to attend. Men naturally want to be the providers.

After packing my wife's lunch the next morning, I drove my son to preschool, forgetting that the route would take me right by my erstwhile employer. I only realized that when the red light stopped me directly across from the office entrance. *Just my luck*, I thought, turning my head away to stare at the convenience store on the other side of the road and pretend to not notice my still-employed ex-colleagues as they happily pulled into work.

I wonder if things can get any worse, I continued, moments before the car behind me slammed into mine.

Ten minutes later we were parked at the convenience store, talking to the responding officer. No one was hurt and damage was minimal, but I winced every time I saw a former colleague pull up for a coffee before starting their day across the street. Each one glanced at me quizzically, certainly having heard that I'd been laid off, probably wondering why the police were questioning me in a location well within sniper range of the office.

Once we'd traded insurance information, I dragged my further wounded ego to the car and called my wife to talk about irony. She preferred to discuss karma, instructing me to go into the store for a Powerball ticket. In a karmic world, she assured me, a lay-off at least *doubles* one's chances of winning big. Whenever some poor slob is interviewed about having won the jackpot, they're saying something like, "And it's a good thing, 'cause I'd just been laid off!" I couldn't argue with her logic – after all, I was a poor slob.

Our ticket didn't win, but I was impressed with her reasoning. We've since established a set of similar rules to cover when/how to purchase lottery tickets. Most of them are based on observation of actual winners' stories; none is based on true statistics or logic. But feel free to try them:

1: Buy your tickets after major, life-changing incidents that pose a serious threat to your family's well-being. If you have six months to live, you will win millions.

2: Let the computer choose your numbers for you. The computer is smarter than you (which is why it never buys lottery tickets). If you're going to win from a bunch of randomly *chosen* numbers, you might as well play randomly *generated* numbers. Besides, rule **2a** says if you choose your own numbers and play them each time, they'll only win big that one week you're too busy to get a ticket.

3: Put your ticket in a place where you'll forget about it for six months or longer. The closer you come to the cut-off date for a pay-out, the more likely it is that you have won the jackpot. If you remember it 45 minutes before the deadline and you live 40 minutes from the nearest claims office, you're about to become a millionaire.

4: When you discover an old ticket in your coat pocket, mail it in without even checking it. Further tempt fate by eschewing certified or insured mail – send it by regular mail two days before the deadline, and you'll be rich by week's end.

5: Buy your tickets at the scariest, nastiest store possible. People don't win jackpots on tickets from those machines you find in squeaky-clean grocery stores built inside gated communities. To buy a big winner, you have to feel genuinely afraid for your life when you get out of your car to go into the store. Your fear may be justified, but your courage will be rewarded.

6: If a store sells a big winner in one game, they'll never sell another in *any* game. They've received their allotment of big winners – one.

7: If you write an article about the lottery, don't buy a ticket until it's published. If I'd won last week, this piece would hardly be as credible as it is.

Please don't assume I'm stupid or bad at math. I understand statistics, so put the phone down, Dad. I know the odds are hopelessly minuscule. People say the odds of winning are the same as the odds of getting struck by lightning. Still, who *doesn't* run like crazy if they're caught outside during a lightning storm?

I also understand the moral objections, but I'm not greedy for merely *hoping* to win. If you *want* money, you're human; if you *love* money, you've crossed a line. I'm safe. I don't love money; I'm just in a really unhealthy relationship with it.

Maybe I've already been punished for that, by an incident that confirmed rule **5** for me. I had a favorite lottery stop near my new job. There are bars on the windows, roaches on the shelves and deadbeats on the sidewalk; there *had* to be a winning scratcher somewhere in this gas station's future.

For months, I drove there every Friday during lunch to buy my favorite scratcher. On my last visit, I was shocked to see a sign proclaiming they'd sold a $250,000 winner. I knew from rule **6** that I shouldn't bother buying anything there, but I was curious about the winner and went inside to chat with the clerk. That's when my ego received a killing blow – news more devastating even than the lay-off had been. The big winner they'd sold had been from the series of scratchers that I'd regularly bought there. They'd sold it the previous Friday, at about the same time I usually buy mine.

So where had I been one week prior, while someone else was winning my quarter mil? Let's just say I've amended the rules...

8: Never call in "sick" on the day you usually buy tickets.

Karma stinks sometimes.

- March/April 2008

Lie Ability Coverage

There is only one quality worse than hardness of heart and that is softness of head.

– Theodore Roosevelt

I've already written about the morning another car plowed into mine while I was stopped at a traffic light. It happened during a particularly rough 24 hours, but we were uninjured, it wasn't my fault and there was no damage to my vehicle – not such a bad outcome, in retrospect.

It was also nearly two years ago, making it old news as far as I'm concerned. Apparently our insurance company feels differently, as evidenced by the email they just sent to inquire about the accident.

I've heard the horror stories and urban legends of insurers raising rates for people who've been hit (but not at fault), arguing that statistically, anyone who's been involved in an accident is in a higher risk group. Which is why my first reaction was, I need to lie through my teeth if I'm going to avoid having my rates raised.

My second reaction was, Boy, these folks are really on the ball – it's only been 23 months since the accident occurred.

My third and final reaction was, Maybe I should send a return email with my actual answers. That might not seem noteworthy, but the questions were so idiotic that I hoped my answers would help the insurers be more careful what they ask for in the future.

Here are their actual questions, with my answers:

Q: A recent Motor Vehicle Report received for Daniel indicates that he was involved in an automobile accident on Wednesday, July 12, 2006. We do not have a record of this accident and would appreciate you providing us with additional information.

A: I don't understand your question, as it was really more of a statement. Perhaps you should have labelled it "S" instead of "Q" – unless this is a true-or-false quiz, in which case my answer is: True – you don't have a record of such an accident. Next question, please.

Q: Please answer the questions on the reverse side of this form and return it in the enclosed envelope within 10 days.

A: Would that be 10 days in regular time, or 10 days in your time? The accident was in July 2006 and it's now June 2008. I'll try to get back to you by May 2010.

Also, can you please direct me to the "reverse side" of this e-mail message? I tried turning my monitor around, but didn't see any additional questions back there. The same goes for the "enclosed envelope" – oddly enough, I haven't found an envelope enclosed in this electronic message. Please e-mail me a new envelope within 10 days.

Q: Time of accident: _____

A: I don't remember, but it was near the start of the workday, because the moron who hit me was rushing to work. He hadn't gotten laid off the night before and I had, yet somehow I was ahead of him in the morning commute.

Q: Was a ticket received?   0 Yes   0 No

A: I'm confused again. Is that a score update? Those are zeros, right? Does that mean the game is tied, nothing all, between the Yes team and the No team?

Or am I expected to fill in one of those to indicate an answer in my e-mail reply? If so, do I have to use a Number 2 non-existent magical cyber-pencil, or will any non-existent magical cyber-pencil do?

Speaking of zeros, that's how many answers I'm able to give, because I have no idea if a ticket was received. I know I didn't receive one because I didn't do anything wrong, but I don't know if the moron received one.

Q: If Yes, what was the ticket for?

A: It was probably for at least $100.

Q: Who was given the ticket? _____

A: If anybody got one, it was the moron. Why don't you go ask him?

Q: Who was at fault?

A: I haven't been calling him "moron" for nothing.

Q: Damage amount to your vehicle $___

A: 0. Which isn't a checkbox. It's a real zero. As in, no damage. As in, no claim. As in, no need for this inquiry.

Q: Damage amount to the other party's vehicle $___

A: No idea. It was none of my business, so I didn't ask. Perhaps you should adopt the same philosophy.

Q: Bodily Injury?   0 Yes   0 No   If Yes, how much $___

A: No, thanks. What kind of sicko do you think I am?

Q: Details of accident: _____

A: Sorry I can't write my answer on the convenient line you've provided in this e-mail message. My cyber-handwriting is big and sloppy, and my written reply would never fit in the space you've provided. So I'll type the details here: I was rear-ended while I was stopped at a red light. My vehicle was un-damaged, but the moron's front end crumpled. Score one for the good guys!

Q: Which insurance company paid for damages? (yours or the other person's)

A: What do you mean by "yours"? Shouldn't that say "us" instead? Wouldn't "yours" to me be *you*? You seem to be trying to disassociate your company from the question. Aren't *you* my insurance company? And if so, shouldn't you already know whether "mine" paid for damages? I'm assuming "you" never paid for damages, because there were none.

As for the "other person's," I have no idea if they paid for anything, because I have no idea if he filed with them. If the damage to his vehicle was low enough, it'd make sense for him not to have filed in order to avoid an increase in rates.

Then again, if "his" insurance company is the same as "mine" then "his" is probably asking him all sorts of irrelevant questions right now, just so "they" can raise his rates, wheth-er they paid for damages or not.

Q: In order to protect your privacy, please do not include personal information such as your driver's license number, social security number, date of birth or financial account details in a reply email.

A: Hold on; you just sent me a two-page, apparent front-and-back e-mail message with numerous personal questions, the answers to which are none of your business. And on the last one, you're suddenly concerned with my privacy?

Why do I have a feeling you let the cavemen write this questionnaire?

- June 2008

Marriage by the Numbers

Before I got married I had six theories about bringing up children; now I have six children, and no theories.

– John Wilmot

In 2001, my siblings and I threw a surprise party in honor of my parents' fiftieth anniversary. At the time, they seemed healthy and spry, but now – eight years, a goiter surgery, a stroke, a Parkinson's diagnosis and a brown recluse bite later – we're beginning to ponder some unpleasant questions.

And so, it would seem, are Mom and Dad – they recently said they want to see North Carolina's Outer Banks "one more time" and I haven't quite recovered from the implications of that. For starters, I hate driving over that bridge.

More importantly, "one more time" sounds too final – it reminds me of my youth, when every December my grandmother would say, "This will probably be my last Christmas." Even though that turned out to be okay – she enjoyed "her last Christmas" for at least seven years – I get uneasy hearing her daughter say similar things now.

So, just to wax morose as well as put things in perspective for Mother's and Father's Day, I dug out the toast I wrote for that party eight years ago. When I wrote it, the right brain I'd inherited from Mom failed me, so I turned to what Dad passed onto me – empirical observation. Perhaps marriage is a science, and love is based on numbers. So I did a little quantitative analysis, and discovered a true legacy in numbers....

My parents have now been married for nearly 58 years. During that time, they had eight children (which means Mom spent six years being pregnant). Eighty-eight percent of their kids were born during 33 percent of the year. That 33 percent of the year happens to fall nine months after the *coldest* 33 percent of the year. For the sake of my own sanity, I refuse to extrapolate further.

As of this year, those eight kids have been alive for a total of 392 years. The resulting 12 grandchildren and great grandchildren represent another 208 years of life, for a total of 600 years of life kick-started by my mom and dad.

Those 20 descendants, meanwhile, have gone on to create another nine marriages – and three divorces. My parents paid good money for both.

During their marriage, my parents have lived in three states, eight towns and ten houses. With nine move-ins and ten move-outs, Mom has run the family vacuum cleaner 19 times – it's still like new!

My parents have owned 13 cars and housed 27 pets – 12 cats (five of which were unceremoniously dumped at one of their ten houses by three of their eight kids), seven dogs, four lizards, two hermit crabs (it started as three, but one didn't survive the trip home from the Outer Banks), one snake and, for a short while, a baby rabbit that I'd discovered injured in the yard. They never knew about that last one; it died a premature death. (By the way, never hide a baby rabbit in a snake's terrarium.)

As of their anniversary, my parents will have spent 21,170 days together, possibly qualifying them for sainthood. At three a day, they've shared 63,510 meals. I think Dad cooked two of them.

Assuming they did so every year for each kid until that kid turned 18, they threw 144 birthday parties. At an average of seven friends attending each, that's 1008 screaming kids who have eaten 72 gallons of ice cream in nine of their ten homes. Add up the years 1 through 18 as a series, and you get 171. Multiply that by eight kids, and you get 1368 – the number of birthday candles they've lit on their children's cakes. Yet remarkably, they never had to use another magic number, 911.

For 34 years, they had a child or children somewhere between grades K and 12. Assuming that lasted 13 years for all eight kids (not a safe assumption in my family), they endured back-to-school shopping 104 times. At 180 days for each school year, Mom packed 18,720 lunches. This required 37,440 slices of bread, 2340 packs of baloney, 1170 packs of cheese and 585 pints of yellow mustard.

From sixth grade on, each of us had six classes a day, or 42 classes over that seven-year span. That's 336 classes over the eight-kid spectrum; if those teachers tried twice a year before giving up, Mom and Dad attended 672 embarrassing parent-teacher conferences. Back then, we had six grading periods each year, amounting to 2016 hidden report cards my parents had to find. This also means 2016 times that they found them, read the results and offered good money for any kid to bring home A's the next time.

Actual funds disbursed? None.

They endured a 39-year span during which there were minors in their home (in fact, for one memorable year, they housed five teenagers, locking up their qualification for sainthood). That's 39 pumpkins carved in October, as well as 39 pulpy masses kicked off the edge of the porch in December. Assuming an average germination rate of five seeds per pumpkin, that's 195 vines they had growing in their front yards in August.

Two dozen times 39 equals 936 Easter eggs they've dyed, thanks to 234 Paas tablets and 702 tablespoons of vinegar. Each kid ate two, leaving eight of the two dozen eggs in the fridge on Easter morning. Over the 39 years, that means Mom found 312 colorful, smelly messes in the back of the fridge some time during the summer or early fall.

At 30 per pack, there were 1170 fuses and/or sparklers ignited over 39 Independence Days. Allow four careless years during each kid's awkward phase, and my parents changed 32 bandages on July 5.

Dad's put up 58 Christmas trees, using pretty much the same lights since 1951. With six strings per tree at 50 fixtures per string, he's switched out approximately 17,400 bulbs before finally finding the burnt-out one.

Remember those 600 years of life? My parents have bought Christmas gifts for all of them. Socks, underwear, a shirt, pants and a toy come to five gifts each, or 3000 boxes they've wrapped. Assuming one tube for each group of five, there have been 12,000 square feet of wrapping paper balled up and tossed onto their living room floors over the years.

I added up our annual vacations and determined that Dad has driven about 65,000 miles' worth of them. At a conservative estimate of 50-mile intervals, that's 1300 "Are we there yet"s, along with 2600 "Don't make me turn this car around"s.

What did it take for them to get through all of those numbers? I had trouble estimating this one, but I'm sure it's expressed in 12-ounce increments.

Beyond that, it all comes down to two – and to those two, I'd just like to say thanks for playing by the numbers. If you promise you'll commit to more than just "one more" Outer Banks trip, I think I can brave that bridge for every one of them.

- May/June 2009

The Poop That Saved Christmas

Diaper backward spells repaid. Think about it.
— Marshall McLuhan

When I told Doodlebug about my latest layoff, I tried to put it in as positive a light as I could and told him when the company merged with another company, they had twice as many people without having twice as much work to do. I stressed that I hadn't done anything wrong and that it was nothing personal, but that they no longer had enough work for me, so I was basically finished with my job.

I said nothing about us having been treated more like an acquisition in spite of the fact that our company owned a controlling share of the merged company's new stock, which was simply a mechanism for our fat cat CEO to make a truckload of money by selling us down the river. I didn't cast aspersions on his greedy ass having cut us loose during the worst economic crisis since the Great Depression, nor did I point out that the company's profits had been up by more than 80 percent this year, thereby negating any argument that the layoffs were a necessary cost-cutting maneuver.

I figured that was too much for a seven-year-old to face, which is also the reason I merely *hinted* that my ex-CEO is going to rot in Hell, rather than saying it outright. Anything else would be an unfair burden to the little guy, so I put on a smile and simply told him I'd be looking for a new job for a little while, ignoring the urge to add that during that time he should ignore any weeping sounds he might hear coming from Mommy and Daddy's room.

Later came the talk of cutting our own expenses. We knew we'd be able to pay all of our bills through the end of the year, with little extra. Unfortunately, that time span includes a period when tradition dictates that a family spend a little extra. I'm talking, of course, about Christmas – one of the two most important holidays on the Christian liturgical calendar, as well as the season to essentially stick a vacuum cleaner hose in my wallet.

This year, we've switched that vacuum cleaner off, and Christmas is suddenly about religion again. That's also difficult for a seven-year-old to accept, but we figured it might be easier if he had advance notice. Hence came Part Two of The Talk, in which I explained that fortunately, we'd bought a few gifts for him and his brother *before* I'd lost my job, my money and my self-worth. This meant they'd get *something* for Christmas, but not nearly as much as in past years.

He took the news remarkably well; in fact, he even put a positive spin on it: "That's okay, Dad – at least Santa Claus will still bring us the big gifts."

After removing that dagger from my heart, I slank to my computer to see if there was any possible excess in the budget I'd worked up. Damn that Santa! He's always upstaging me. But I might have the last laugh, as the budget review yielded no chance for Santa to come through.

There's another aspect of the holidays that was affected by the layoff – travel. My parents live in Northern Virginia, and we need to visit them. Especially since my mom had a stroke last month. Even more especially, since she hallucinated that we were there for a visit while she was hospitalized.

Little aside here – the news of Mom's stroke was the third bad thing to happen in one week. The layoff was second, and the first was the death of a long-time pet. It wasn't my favorite week on the calendar, but what really upset me was that it started, literally, within minutes of my having attempted to help my church.

My priest had asked me to write this year's stewardship letter. He wanted me to urge our parishioners to increase their financial pledges in the coming year, so I wrote a heartfelt missive on how it's necessary to make sacrifices in order to receive blessings. I wrote about how my family has been abundantly blessed every time we've increased our pledge, and urged my fellow parishioners to do the same.

I'm guessing, though, that we haven't been giving enough ourselves. I admit it hasn't been the Biblical standard of one full bale of wheat for every nine we've put aside. Sadly, we usually give a handful of grains. For me to ask the rest of the congregation to tithe probably amounted to new heights of hypocrisy, and there are some lines you just don't cross with God. To put it lightly, I think I ticked Him off.

Because as soon as I emailed the draft of that letter, my cat's health took a turn for the worse, and she was dead by evening. About the same time the church secretary finished mailing the letters, I was receiving a little phone call from HR, telling me not to bother coming in the next day. And as the letter was being delivered to most of the parishioners' homes, I was getting the news of my mom's sudden onset of temporary paralysis.

Message received, God. You've had it up to there with me, and this has been payback time. It cost me my cat, my job, and nearly my mom. She's recovering and we're getting over the cat, but the job thing really hurt. Can it be a coincidence that the most prolifically screwed person from the Old Testament spelled his name J-o-b?

Aside complete.

We knew we should go visit my parents in Virginia during the holidays. Thankfully, Mom is back at the house, but for us to get there would have cost more than we have right now. It's not enough for the price of gas to have come down; unfortunately, we need to stay in a hotel. My parents' dog sends our allergies off the scale, so we can't spend the night in their house without at least three of us waking up choking on our own snot.

Not so with my in-laws. They do nothing to affect my snot production; the only bodily fluid in question when we get together is the amount of bile we manage to raise in each other.

Which is why we chose to visit *them* for Thanksgiving. They live a little closer, so the gas cost is better, but the big difference is in being able to sleep in their house instead of a hotel. But halfway there, I started feeling the guilt about my own parents.

"Are we going to try to go to Virginia over the holidays, too?" my wife asked in the dark of the car. I ignored the question and kept typing on my laptop.

"Dan?" I think she thought I hadn't heard her. Looked like I was going to have to answer her.

"I don't know," I sighed. "I just don't see how we can afford it right now. We can't even afford to buy them presents, let alone stay at a hotel so we can see them. I'm still wondering how we're going to afford presents for the boys."

"Daddy?" Uh-oh. The three-year-old must have heard me, and was going to voice his objections.

"Yes, Sugarbear?"

"I needa go poo-poo." ('Uh-oh' was right.)

"Okay, hold on. We need to find an exit. Will you sit on the potty at a gas station?"

"No. Puyyup."

Sigh. We've been 50 percent successful with his potty training so far. He mostly wears "big boy unnerwear" and is able to keep them dry, but when it comes to Number Two, he's been defiantly resistant. He warns us when it's on its way, but refuses to sit on a potty.

Instead, we have to take off his pants and underwear, put on a Pull-Up, and let him do his business as if he's still in diapers. He calls them "puyyups," pronouncing it the same way you'd pronounce "pollo" in Spanish – remember that the next time you're tempted to order a chicken enchilada. (Aside complete.)

We hit the first exit that had anything listed on a blue sign at the side of I-40 (this was during that desolate stretch of swampland that seems to last all the way from Raleigh to Wilmington), pulled up behind the closest convenience store and made ready for the deed.

The multiple disrobings necessary for Sugarbear's preferred elimination method require that he temporarily stand in his socks and leave his pants on the floor; because we would have to be insane to do that on the floor of a gas station restroom, we decided to attempt his routine in the car. One parent would have to get in the back with him, so the front seats would have to be pushed forward far enough to accommodate them. This meant the other parent would have to get out of the way by waiting outside the car.

My wife was willing to do the hard part while I stood in the 20-degree night, waiting for her to roll down the window and hand me a sealed freezer bag containing a soiled Pull-Up and wipes. My job was to throw it away while she changed him back into his big boy underwear in the warmth and relative safety of the car.

While I shivered and waited, I watched as a drunk stumbled across the parking lot to a private spot behind the dumpster. He came back a minute later, and I figured he hadn't wanted to risk the public restroom, either. I'm not sure what he left back there, but I knew there was no way I was going anywhere near that dumpster.

Which meant that when I finally took possession of the freezer bag, I had to walk around to the front of the store to find a trashcan for it. I couldn't find one, so I thought of instead keeping the bag in order to mail it to my former CEO.

But I was resolute and my search took me inside the convenience store. I forgot all about the freezer bag once I noticed the glitzy display of lottery scratchers at the cash register. When I remembered my own lottery rules – including the increased likelihood of winning when a ticket is purchased in a nasty store in the middle of nowhere – I knew I had to buy one.

So I sidled up to the counter and asked for one of the scratchers, fishing in my wallet for the right bill. I didn't have exact change, so I laid a bigger bill on the counter. The cashier saw it and asked if I was sure I didn't want to buy two scratchers. I smiled and told her no, I shouldn't even be buying one, but if it was a lucky one, I'd take it. She promised me it was a winner, gave me my change, and wished me a Happy Thanksgiving. As I returned the sentiment, I glanced at her nametag. "Virginia." Ouch. Let the guilt continue.

I ran back into the cold and headed for the car, concerned that the drunk might be pestering my family. If he had been, I simply would have asked him for money in order to run him off. He was nowhere to be seen, so I jumped into the car, dropping the freezer bag and lottery ticket at my feet as I buckled up and we headed for the Interstate again.

We arrived in our usual flurry of chaos, the boys hyped on chocolate and excited about seeing their grandparents, me unloading our luggage as quickly as possible in order to minimize my risk of hypothermia. When all was said and done, it wasn't until the next morning that I remembered the scratcher.

My wife was out window-shopping with her mother and the boys were messing around in the garage with my father-in-law. I took advantage of the quiet to sneak a piece of cake and a glass of milk, then went to the car to look for my lottery ticket and a coin to scratch it with.

I found a penny and began the anticipatory scratching ritual. I won $200 on the first space and was ecstatic. I figured I wasn't likely to win any more than that, but continued scratching anyway. Nothing. Nothing. $100. The holidays were suddenly looking up!

Next space, nothing. Then $100 again. Then a third $100. Was this really a $500 winner, or was I reading the numbers wrong?

Next two spaces, nothing. Then another $200. Whoa. They don't make $700 winners, do they?

Nope – next space, another $200! Nothing, nothing, then end nicely with $100 in the last space.

When I called my wife to tell her we'd just won $1000, she asked, "How is that possible?" That's when I had to admit I'd been frivolous and bought a lottery ticket, but I hoped she wasn't mad. She wasn't.

She asked where I'd bought the ticket, and that's when it hit me – I had no idea where. Neither one of us could remember the exit number, the town, the highway, the gas company or the store name. It was supposed to have been nothing but a poop stop, but suddenly my son had presented us with the richest poop in town. Courtesy of a cashier named ... *Virginia*.

"Sweetie, maybe we should visit my parents during the holidays, after all. Now we can afford a hotel for a night."

"Okay."

"And maybe we should buy a couple more presents for the boys."

"Okay."

"And what the heck? Why not make a mortgage payment, while we're at it?"

"Okay."

"You okay?"

"Okay."

"See you when you get back; love you!"

"Okay."

I hung up, promising myself I'd never get mad at Sugar-bear again. It didn't take long to break that resolution, but we're sticking with the others. We're going to see my parents and we're getting a couple of nicer presents for the boys. And sure, the mortgage thing, too.

This week, I've been thinking maybe God is okay with me again. But tonight He sent me another message. Christmas is saved, but I still have more poop to go through before I am...

Today we dragged the artificial tree out of the outside storage closet and shook out the spider webs. After we assembled the three sections, I plugged in the tree and discovered one string of lights wasn't working. Nothing new about that; we lose a bulb or two every year. I just had to find the empty socket and put in a new bulb.

I was rustling through a particularly thick clump of plastic pine needles when wham! Something put an absolute clampdown on my arm. I've never felt pain like this before; it started in my wrist and shot all the way up to my shoulder.

I pulled my hand out and checked my wrist, where I saw two little black pinpoints. Terrific. I was pretty sure I'd just been bitten by a brown recluse spider, and now my arm was going to have to be amputated.

But when I tried to find the spider to exact my revenge, I instead discovered the source of the faulty string – not an empty socket, but a broken bulb. Its exposed wires were the same distance apart as the two throbbing marks on my wrist.

My Christmas tree had actually shocked me. One of the nicest, prettiest things about the holidays, and it had damn near killed me. Message received loud and clear, God, and I'm sorry. I can reform.

Maybe I'll start by throwing away that freezer bag before the mail truck shows up....

- November 2008

123

A Nay for Effort

Afternoon Dismissal

Only a narcissist would quote himself.
— Dan Bain

About the Author

courtesy April Maness

Dan Bain is a humor writer, improv comedian and emcee from Raleigh, North Carolina. His column Bain's Beat has won multiple state and national awards, earning him a fan base from one end of his couch to the other. Dan has written professionally since 1995, both as a freelancer and as a corporate drone. His work has appeared in The Raleigh News & Observer, Midtown Magazine, Cary Living, Pinehurst Magazine, America's Funniest Humor and Chicken Soup for the Soul. Dan hates writing about himself in the third person. For additional useless information about Dan, please see **www.danbain.net**. For the most important information, please see the following paragraph:

In much-needed contrition and with a secret hope to one day prove to his beleaguered ex-teachers that he did, too, amount to something, Dan will give 10 percent of this book's profit back to them, so thanks for buying it. The contributions will go to various schools and organizations that support teachers and their mission; a comprehensive list will be updated on Dan's website as the donations take place.

The world is hurting.
Laugh more.

Made in the USA
Middletown, DE
23 January 2022

59469315R00083